Sit or Serve?

Brenda Troutman

Sit or Serve?

Discovering How to Balance
Our Mary and Martha

Brenda Troutman

RIVER BIRCH PRESS

Mesa, Arizona

ISBN 978-1-956365-70-2 (print)
ISBN 978-1-956365-71-9 (e-book)

For Worldwide Distribution
Printed in the U.S.A.

River Birch Press
P.O. Box 7341, Mesa, AZ 85216

*This book is dedicated to my mother, Sandy Galentine,
who has been such a good example of someone
who has found the balance between her Mary and Martha.
She has a sacrificial love like no one else I know.*

Contents

Acknowledgments

I would like to first thank my Lord and Savior Jesus Christ. It is only through Him that I am able to do anything, and I thank Him for giving me this gift of writing.

I also would like to thank my husband, Chris, for always standing by my side and supporting me as I follow my dreams.

Thanks to Michele Huey, who has supported me, given me advice, and guided me on this writing journey.

Finally thank you to my church and work families for the support and encouragement you have given me through this crazy journey of life.

Preface

Finding balance in our lives can be a struggle. We have to learn how to balance our work with our leisure time, our activities with time to rest, and our responsibilities with time to let loose and have fun. Even though it can be difficult, maintaining this balance in our lives is important to our physical, mental, and emotional health.

In searching for this peace and stability, it is also important that we don't neglect our spiritual health. We find this struggle for balance in Scripture in the home of Mary and Martha, where the two women find themselves in a conflict over whether to sit at the Lord's feet or serve Him.

As Christians, especially in today's busy culture, we find it difficult to sit quietly before the Lord. Listening to His voice has become a challenging task because we have forgotten how to hear Him. It seems as if we think that if we are not on the move, we are not being productive.

It is evident throughout Scripture, but particularly in the account of Mary and Martha, that Jesus says quiet time with Him needs to be the first priority if we are going to serve Him well. Through this book, I hope we learn together the importance of being still before Him.

While sharing this lesson of finding quiet time, we can't forget that the Lord also emphasizes the importance of serving Him. That is why the subtitle to this book is "Discovering How to Balance Our Mary and Martha." Both acts—sitting at His feet and serving Him—are important in our spiritual walk. Too many times I think that Martha is given a bad reputation because she didn't choose to sit at Jesus' feet. Did she need to sit at His feet and learn from Him? Absolutely. But does that mean her service wasn't important? Absolutely not.

These two principles are practices that I have had to develop in my own life, but I am certainly not perfect at living them out. I have made a habit of having quiet devotional time every morning, though I must confess sometimes my mind gets distracted. For over twenty years, I have worked in Christian education, taught Sunday school, and served on my church's worship team. These are all acts of service that I thoroughly enjoy, and they give me an opportunity to use the gifts God has given me.

There have been times, though, when these acts of service have become more of an obligation than an act of worship. I have felt the urge, as wrong as it is, to point out other people who are not serving and say, "Why aren't they helping?" It is during those times that I most need to sit at the feet of Jesus and have Him show me the better way. You see, serving Jesus is important, and it is a great source of joy, but my relationship with Jesus is far more important. When that relationship is neglected, the service becomes a burden, not a joy.

As we see ourselves through the story of these two women and understand just how beautiful and valued we are in the eyes of our Lord, let's also realize how much He wants us to find the perfect rest that only He can provide. As we observe how each person in this account felt and responded to each other, let's put ourselves in their shoes and learn from them.

Use the questions and scriptures found on the pages at the end of each chapter to reflect on what you have read and discovered. Take to heart the ideas that come to you as you read, then go and live them out. It would be beneficial to find a partner or small group with whom you can study and talk through what you've learned.

Let's allow our thinking to become transformed through spending time with Jesus and experience the delight we can have in serving Him when our focus is in the right place. Remember, it doesn't matter what everyone else thinks you should be doing;

Jesus knows better. Remember not to let others dictate how you should be serving the Lord.

Instead, allow Jesus to show you His plan for your journey with Him. And most of all, remember to take time out of the busyness of life to simply sit at Jesus' feet and let Him teach you. Be sure, like these two women, to discover the balanced life that Jesus has to offer.

Introduction

We live in a hurry-up, always-stay-busy kind of society. Everything we desire is almost instantly at our fingertips. We rarely have to wait for anything. We have microwaves to make our food in seconds or minutes, smart phones that can give us access to information 24/7, and even social media to make sure we are keeping up with everyone else's lives as well as our own. Anything we want to buy is easily accessible and sometimes can be purchased and delivered the same day.

We constantly juggle all the things we need to do...but we don't do most of them well. We are consumed by work and entertainment, so much so that we forget to just sit and bask in the Lord's goodness. When we aren't working, there is always a game to play on our phones or a television show that we just can't miss. Add in our hobbies, and we have filled up all of our available time. As Christians, we also have this sense of having to "do" more for the Lord. Serving the Lord is important, but not when it causes us to neglect our relationship with Him.

Through the account of Mary and Martha, let's take a step back and see how Jesus desires us to live. The constant busyness is not healthy physically, emotionally, or spiritually. Jesus knows how our priorities should be lined up and desires to help us. He wants us to unlearn these habits of always needing to be busy, always needing to be entertained, and never taking the time to be made whole.

We need to learn how to put down the burdens and distractions of life to quietly seek Him and sit at His feet. To do this will require us to transform the way we think. As it says in Romans 12:2, "Do not conform to the pattern of this world, but be transformed by the renewing of your mind. Then you will be able to test and approve what God's will is—his good, pleasing and perfect will."

Martha was a woman who needed to learn this lesson. When Jesus visited the home of Martha and her sister Mary, Martha so desperately wanted to serve Him that she missed what was more important—resting with Him. I want us to understand that her service to the Lord was valued and important; she simply needed to work on the condition of her heart so her service would be fulfilling.

While studying this event in Scripture, sit back and learn that, while both women were doing something important, Jesus said that one of them found what was better. Sit still and grasp that same sense of sitting at the feet of Jesus because He promises that what you find won't be taken from you. Our walk with Jesus is better when we find the balance between sitting at His feet and serving Him.

Take some time to read Luke 10:38-42. Sit with every character and consider what they would have been thinking and feeling. Before continuing to read this book, reflect on how you tend to be like each of the two women. Take some time to pray and ask God to teach you through studying this passage deeper. Then allow me to invite you into the home of these two sisters. Let's sit together at their table for a while and allow Jesus to show us how to balance our lives with Him.

1

Open Your Life to Jesus

As Jesus and his disciples were on their way, he came to a village where a woman named Martha opened her home to him (Luke 10:38).

Jesus was not a man who stayed in one place for any length of time. In this opening line of the account of Mary and Martha, we see Him moving from village to village as He always did, ministering to people. Remember, Jesus Himself had no physical home, but often used the homes of people in the towns He passed through to sit with them and care for them.

We often see Jesus sitting at a table in somebody's house. So many times He is there, not to gain sustenance and rest for Himself, but to teach the people in that household something with eternal significance. Such was the case with Mary and Martha, but the first step was Martha inviting Him in. Jesus can't minister to a closed door.

Unexpected Company

If you read through the rest of the account, it seems as though Martha was not expecting company. After inviting Jesus into her home, she became very busy and distracted with all of the preparations that had to be made in order to make sure her guest was comfortable and provided for.

She became so busy, in fact, that she almost missed the best

1

part of the visit—Jesus Himself. In later chapters, we'll examine what Jesus wanted to teach her in this moment, but there is something we can learn just by the fact that she opened the door. Even though she thought she was not ready for company—the house needed straightening and food needed to be made—she invited Him in anyway.

Have you ever found yourself in this situation? Your house is clean, but not the kind of clean it would be if you were expecting company. You know the drill. When guests are coming to visit, you inspect every inch of your house to make sure everything is in its proper place. No dust is on the shelves, no dishes in the sink, no crumbs on the table. You want to make sure that your guests feel comfortable and welcome, so everything needs to be perfect.

If you're providing some kind of food, it has to be prepared in advance and cooked exactly right. You make sure your own appearance is neat and tidy, too, by taking the time to dress nicely and fix your hair. When the guests arrive, everything is prepared and ready, not a thing is missing. You have worked, and you are going to provide the best atmosphere possible.

What happens, though, when that doorbell rings unexpectedly? Do you find yourself looking around the house at those little messes that show that your house is actually lived in, mortified that your guests will see something imperfect? Or do you look down at what you are wearing and think, *I can't possibly answer the door looking like this!* How often do we open the door to that unexpected call and find ourselves moving briskly to fix things instead of just enjoying the company of whomever it was that came knocking?

I confess—this is me. While I keep a clean house, there are times that I allow the little messes of life to wait while I relax and read a book or watch TV. But when the doorbell rings, I go into panic mode. It's as if I think that everybody else has their house in perfect condition at all times, and I can't possibly let someone in when my house isn't in that same state of perfection.

How could company enjoy their visit when my house is messy, and I'm in sweatpants, wearing my hair in a ponytail? I forget that my guest has come to see *me*, not the state of my house or what I'm wearing that day. Jesus comes to do the same—to spend time with you without worrying about you fixing everything first.

Whitewashing Tombs

Let's take an honest look at how, whether preparing for expected guests or the anxiety that comes with unexpected ones, our actions are about keeping up appearances. We somehow have this perception that everybody lives this perfect, tidy life except for us. We overlook the fact that what we see on the outside— perfect smiles on social media profiles and public smiles and niceties—are not the whole picture.

The reality is that everyone has messes. Nobody is perfect. Yet we somehow have this need for people to believe that we are perfect—that we have it all together and not a thing is out of place.

This attitude of keeping up appearances is not what Jesus wants for us. In fact, He preached against it in some pretty straightforward messages to the Pharisees and teachers of the law. In Matthew 23:13-36, Jesus had some harsh things to say to this group of people. In particular, in verses 25-28, He said that they "clean the outside of the cup, but the inside is full of greed and self-indulgence."

Jesus then went on to say that these religious leaders were "whitewashed tombs," beautiful on the outside but filled with death on the inside. All these people weren't perfect, as they wanted people to believe. They were putting up a hypocritical façade, making themselves look perfect. They were actually hurting other people with their behavior. Even their own eternal salvation was in jeopardy.

I don't mean to say that Martha was like the Pharisees and teachers of the law, who were taking their status as religious leaders and using it to lord it over the people. Neither are we. However, if we take an honest look at ourselves, I think we will see times when we have missed great opportunities to fellowship and minister to other believers because we were too worried about "the outside of the cup." There are probably times when we could have been ministered to, but again, keeping up appearances got in the way. So many times in our lives, Jesus wants to come in and share something with us, but we are too busy whitewashing our tombs to hear Him.

Letting Jesus In

Now look back at what was happening with Martha. Jesus had come into town, and she wasn't ready for company. She opened the door to let Him in, but there was much to do to make sure that His visit was pleasant. She couldn't possibly stop and sit with Him until everything was in its proper place. She had to straighten up the house and prepare some food to put in front of Him.

In that day, when hospitality was of the utmost importance, Martha would never have allowed a guest to come into her home and not provide for him. The custom of the times was that when a traveler, even a stranger, passed through your village, you opened your home to him. But Jesus was no ordinary traveler, and Martha knew that. So don't miss the significance of the first line of this account: Martha was not prepared for Jesus; she didn't have it all together, but she invited Him in anyway. She opened the door and allowed Jesus into her imperfection.

This is exactly what Jesus wants from us. So often we think that we need to have our lives completely in order, and then we can let Jesus in. We get it so backwards. We think that we have to clean up our lives and make changes so that we will be more acceptable to Him. The reality is that Jesus wants to step right into our mess and clean it up for us. He wants to be the change that cleans up our lives from the inside out. There is no disorder, chaos, or confusion that Jesus can't make beautiful again. So realize that, even if you're not ready, even if you're not cleaned up, Jesus is ready. He is ready to step right into whatever mess you are in. You just need to open that door and let Him in.

Opening the door isn't just a one-time action, however. We do need to open the door to Jesus the first time and receive our eternal salvation from Him. Then, once we're born again, we receive His Holy Spirit. He is with us always and will never leave us nor forsake us, but we need to be sure we invite Him into every situation we face. Too often believers think of inviting Jesus in as a one-and-done event as it applies to gaining the salvation of our souls and forget that we also need daily renewal.

Cleaning Up the Mess

Life doesn't stop being messy after we've trusted in Jesus. But now we have hope that once Jesus is there, He will help us clean up our lives. We still live in this fallen world, the world of which Jesus said, "In this life you will have trouble" (John 16:33). The problems and complexities of life don't disappear just because we are saved. Don't miss the second part of the verse above, "But take heart! I have overcome the world." Jesus has overcome all of the troubles of this world, so we can too. Not in our own power, but in His.

We so often try to solve a problem in our lives in this way: we sit and think through all of the possible scenarios that could make things better. We choose the scenario that we think will provide the best possible solution, the one that will work in our favor. We list all of the pros and cons and decide on the solution that we think is best. Then we ask God to help us as we apply that solution to the problem. We figure out how to fix the mess, and then we ask God to bless us as we fix it.

Do you see how many times the word "we" is used in that process? We think; we choose; we decide. Then we ask God to bless all of it. We get everything figured out our way, and then we invite Jesus in to walk us through our plan. We package up the solution with a nice shiny bow, get it all together, and expect God to bless our way of doing things.

How backwards that is! Our first step should be inviting Jesus into the mess, starting at the beginning. We should ask Him to show us how to fix it, and let Him work. Typically, our own solution isn't the best anyway, and sometimes it just makes the mess bigger.

Consider the example of David. He had gotten himself into a big predicament, and when he tried to fix it himself, the situation just got worse. In 2 Samuel 11, David saw Bathsheba, the wife of Uriah, bathing on the rooftop. He was so enthralled by her that he sent for her and committed adultery with her while her husband was away in battle. Bathsheba became pregnant from this encounter.

Talk about a mess! Right then, David could have repented, asked the Lord for forgiveness, and allowed Him to work out the problem. David still would have had to pay the consequences of his sin, but the problem would not have grown.

However, instead of repenting and asking God what he should do, David tried to fix the problem in his own way. He tried to get Uriah to come home from battle so that he could be with his wife, and then nobody would know that the baby was David's.

Uriah did come home, but he would not lie with his wife, saying that it wouldn't be right for him to come home and enjoy his wife while the other soldiers were still suffering on the battlefield. Instead, he slept with the servants at the entrance to the palace.

David even tried getting Uriah drunk so that he would go sleep with his wife, but that didn't work either. Since that plan failed, David had Uriah placed on the front lines of the battle so that he would be killed. Once her husband was dead, David took Bathsheba home as his wife.

Problem solved. It would look like Uriah died in battle, and nobody would know that Bathsheba had become pregnant before David took her home to be his wife. But the problem wasn't solved. Look at the last sentence in 2 Samuel 11: "But the thing David had done displeased the Lord."

This statement says so much. Yes, David's sin displeased the Lord. But I think the Lord was displeased with much more than the sin. He was displeased that David, when he first saw Bathsheba, didn't invite the Lord in to keep him from sinning. He was displeased that, once David had taken Bathsheba, he didn't call on the Lord and repent right away.

The Lord was displeased that David tried to find his own solution to the mess he had made instead of inviting the Lord in. And he was displeased because David had caused a man to be killed because he was trying to hide his sin instead of confessing it and letting God work. What a tangled mess we get into when we make our own decisions and only do what we think is best for us instead of inviting the Lord in to help. Even David, the man after God's own heart, fell into this trap.

Mary, Martha, and Us

Martha's mess wasn't nearly as big as David's, and yours might not be either. But no matter the size of the mess, Jesus wants to come into it and teach you something. Martha had so much to learn. Knowing that her sister was doing the right thing by sitting at the feet of Jesus, we often come down hard on Martha for being so worried about the preparations and missing out on time with Jesus.

But remember, it was Martha who opened the door. It was Martha who invited Jesus in, even though she wasn't ready for company. Without this first step, she wouldn't have had the opportunity to learn all that Jesus had to teach her. Through her trying to clean up and make the house presentable for company, Jesus was going to show her so much. And there are some tremendous lessons for us to learn from this encounter as well.

Before we move on to see what Jesus was teaching through this meeting with Mary and Martha, take a moment to examine your own life. Have you been trying to keep up appearances with Jesus? Are there decisions that you need to make? Are you finding yourself in the middle of a mess that you don't know how to clean up? Do you feel uncertain about what path to take or how to resolve a conflict with someone? Have you been tossing around scenarios in your mind about what to do?

If the answer to any of those questions is a yes, it's time to open the door and let Jesus into the mess. Don't get it backwards. Don't think that you must figure out the best solution to your problem on your own and then ask God to bless it. Instead, stop rationalizing, stop listing pros and cons, stop dwelling on the problem, and open the door for Jesus. Don't get everything prepared and then ask Him in. Open the door first, invite Him in, and see what He has to show you. Allow Him to work on your behalf.

Let's allow ourselves to go through that door into the home of Martha and Mary. Let's stay in the room and watch the encounters that take place. There are so many lessons packed into the next four verses of this account. Read on, follow Jesus into the home of these two women, and see how He can show you what is better.

Balance Your Mary and Martha

Sit at His Feet

Take some time to sit quietly with Jesus. Ask Him in what ways you need to let Him in. Do you need to take the step of accepting Him as your Savior? Do you need to stop "cleaning up" before you allow Him into your situation? Maybe you need to let go of your own ideas and get answers from Him. Sit at His feet and let Him instruct you where you need to let Him into your life.

Meditate on the following verses as you sit at His feet:

- John 16:33 – "I have told you these things, so that in me you may have peace."

- Romans 10:9 – "If you declare with your mouth, 'Jesus is Lord,' and believe in your heart that God raised him from the dead, you will be saved."

- John 1:12 – "Yet to all who did receive him…he gave the right to become children of God."

Learn from Him

Take some time to think about and journal what you read in this chapter. Use the following questions to guide your thoughts.

- Why was Martha's act of opening the door to Jesus so significant?

- Why is it so important for us to open the door of our lives to Jesus on a daily, even moment-by-moment basis?

- What can you learn from David, who found himself in a mess and then tried to fix it with his own wisdom?

Serve Him

Sometimes the best service you can offer Jesus is just to let go and let Him work. Think about the areas He revealed to you in the time you sat with Him, and journal what you need to let go of and how you will do that.

Put these passages of Scripture into practice as you serve Him:

- 1 Peter 5:7 – "Cast all your anxiety on him because he cares for you."

- James 4:7 – "Submit yourselves, then, to God. Resist the devil, and he will flee from you."

- Philippians 4:6 – "Do not be anxious about anything, but in every situation, by prayer and petition, with thanksgiving, present your requests to God."

2

Sit at His Feet

She had a sister called Mary, who sat at the Lord's feet listening to what he said (Luke 10:39).

After Martha opened the door and let Jesus in, her sister Mary sat at the Lord's feet. There most likely would have been a table in the house for them to sit around and visit, but Mary chose to sit at His feet instead. Sitting at someone's feet means that you are showing submission, that you admire the person, and recognize that you have a lot to learn from the person, or that the person is of higher status than you. Mary clearly recognized that it was Jesus who came into the house that day, and she wasn't going to miss her opportunity to learn from Him.

Recall the flurry of activity that Martha was in. She was not prepared for company, and so Martha was busy trying to make everything perfect for Jesus' visit. It wasn't that Martha didn't recognize who had come to the door that day. She knew that this was Jesus, and she wanted to serve Him. She was very zealous about that.

I'm sure that Mary also recognized that the house wasn't ready for company. It didn't escape her attention that food needed to be prepared and the house straightened up for their guest. So why did she sit down instead of getting things ready with her sister? Mary recognized the more important activity: still, quiet, reverent time at the Master's feet.

At His Feet

There are many instances throughout Scripture in which someone was found at the feet of Jesus. In one particular passage, Luke 8:26-48, there are three different people we see at the feet of Jesus. Let's explore how and why they found themselves there.

First, in verse 35, the people in the area observed a man who had been demon possessed. Jesus had healed him, and he was sitting at Jesus' feet. This man had been living among the tombs, naked and homeless, tormented by demons. In fact, when Jesus asked the demon for his name, the answer was "Legion" because multiple demons possessed the man.

Reading this same account in Mark 5, we see that nobody could approach this man. They had tried putting him in chains, but he would break them to pieces, and nobody could overpower him. So distressed was he that "night and day among the tombs and in the hills he would cry out and cut himself with stones" (Mark 5:5).

Then Jesus walked into his life, sent the demons into a herd of pigs, and the man was healed. He was freed from the torment of these demons that had lived with him for so long. Then he sat at the feet of Jesus, worshipping and learning from Him.

Return to Luke 8, starting in verse 41, and you will see Jairus, a synagogue ruler, falling at the feet of Jesus and pleading for his daughter's life. His daughter, his only daughter, who was just twelve years old, was dying. Imagine the anguish of this man, knowing that the only hope his daughter had was a miracle.

He recognized exactly where he could find this miracle, and so went to seek Jesus. While he was still there with the crowd, in verse 49, Jairus learned that his daughter had died. It was too late. But Jesus said, "Don't be afraid, just believe, and she will be healed." But falling at the feet of Jesus and pleading for mercy was the beginning of this miracle.

In the middle of this event with Jairus, in verses 43-48, a woman who had been subject to bleeding for twelve years touched the hem of Jesus' robe. She had so much faith that she knew if she could just reach out and touch even the hem of His garment, she would be healed. I imagine her lying on the road in desperation, reaching out with all the effort she had, knowing that all she needed to do was grasp that garment as Jesus went by. And when she did, her healing happened instantly.

No more bleeding, no more being an outcast and called unclean because of her condition—just healed. And in verse 47, when she saw that Jesus knew healing power had come out of Him and she wasn't going to just be able to quietly sneak away, she came and fell at His feet, trembling in confession and worship.

The Purpose for Sitting at His Feet

All of these people had one thing in common. They desperately needed a healing touch from the Savior. In the case of the demon possessed man, he sat at Jesus' feet after he was healed, clothed, and restored. I can only imagine what he was feeling and thinking as he sat there whole, listening to Jesus teach him.

Jairus was at Jesus' feet before the healing. He had come to Jesus in desperation, pleading for his daughter's life, and Jesus answered. Finally, the woman who had been subject to bleeding fell at the feet of Jesus after she was healed, confessing to the crowd that Jesus had healed her and worshiping Him with trembling. All of these people were at the feet of Jesus in reverence and awe, and with the knowledge that He could do all things.

Now let's return to Luke 10:39. Here was Mary, at the feet of Jesus. And why was she there? She was listening to what He said. Even with the house needing to be put in perfect order, even with food needing to be prepared, she knew that what Jesus had to say was more important. She had found the only thing that was necessary to receive the healing of her heart—Jesus—and she wasn't going to miss this opportunity to learn from Him.

Let's look at our own lives. Every day, there are so many activities on our agendas. Many of us have a rigid schedule that we have to live by. Maybe you have to be at work during certain hours of the day. You might be juggling your kids' schedules. There are houses to clean and bills to pay. There are ministries that you are involved in at church that demand your time.

Then there are always the unexpected things that pop up in life: the car needs to be repaired, someone in the family gets sick, an appliance in the house breaks and needs to be replaced. On top of all of this, you must try to eat right, exercise, and take care of yourself. None of these things are bad—they are just part of life. But in the middle of it all, do you find time to sit at Jesus' feet? Do you make room to just be still and listen to what He has to say? Let's explore some ways to overcome the obstacles in our way and put this into practice.

Overcoming Obstacles

One obstacle that needs to be overcome is this: we can't see Jesus. All the people we've mentioned so far had Jesus physically present with them. They could see Him, touch Him, and talk face to face with Him. Those of us who have put our faith in Jesus have the Holy Spirit present with us at all times.

We, however, are so used to conversations being face to face with physical people that it can be difficult to learn how to have a conversation with someone we can't see. And honestly, if you haven't been talking with the Lord consistently, it can feel awkward at first. The key is to get in tune with the Holy Spirit so that you *can* talk with Him.

One great way to connect with the Holy Spirit is through worship. Play a worship song and let the lyrics become a prayer.

Close your eyes and listen intently to the words of the song and then sing them back to God yourself. So often the lyrics from worship songs are words from Scripture, so you are actually singing God's Word back to Him. That leads to another means of getting in tune with the Holy Spirit: the words of Scripture.

Find God's promises and repeat them back to Him. Pray like Moses in Exodus 32:13 when he said, "Remember your servants Abraham, Isaac and Israel, to whom you swore by your own self: 'I will make your descendants as numerous as the stars in the sky and I will give your descendants all this land I promised them, and it will be their inheritance forever.'"

It's not as if God forgot His promise; He doesn't forget anything. By praying His promises back to Him, you are acknowledging your belief in those promises. If you're having a hard time sensing His presence, start by praying the promise that He will never leave you nor forsake you (Deuteronomy 31:6; Hebrews 13:5).

This does take some getting used to. After all, you are talking to someone who you know is there, but you can't see Him with your physical eyes. Don't get discouraged if you can't sense Him right away. Just rest in the promise that He will always be there (Matthew 28:20). Once you and the Lord have settled in your spirit that He is there, then determine, like Mary, to sit quietly at His feet and listen to what He has to say.

Learning to listen to Him, however, is another obstacle because again, we won't be able to listen with our physical ears. Do I believe that God can speak audibly if He wants to? Absolutely. But His voice to our spirits usually doesn't reach us in that way. He does speak, but we need to know how to listen. Remember this from John 10:27: "My sheep listen to my voice; I know them, and they follow me." If you are His sheep, His child, you will be able to listen and hear His voice.

Often, the Lord speaks through His Word. Choose a passage

of Scripture, even if it's only a verse or two. Read it and reread it, and then sit quietly and ask the Lord what He has to say to you through that passage. The Holy Spirit can also speak through song.

Remember we learned previously that worship songs often quote Scripture, so that is just one more way to meditate on the Word and hear God's voice. The Lord can also speak through other believers. There are times that someone says the perfect words at just the right time, exactly what you needed to hear in that moment. That is the Holy Spirit speaking to your spirit.

Finally, nature itself declares the glory of God. Take some time to read through Psalm 148 to see all of the wonderful ways nature praises God. Then get to a place outside that is quiet, where you can hear the sounds of nature and praise God along with His Creation. Remember that you are part of that glorious Creation, and He can speak to your spirit when you are sitting still before Him, praising Him along with all of the other amazing things He has created.

A third obstacle, one that you have almost complete control over, is time. Every one of us is given the same 24-hour day, and we get to choose how to spend every second of it. I know that life is busy; we have jobs, families, obligations, hobbies—so many matters that take up our time.

Sometimes we get so focused on what we *have* to do that we don't realize that we could have said no to many of those activities. Now we feel obligated to do them. There are also things we don't have control over, such as our work schedule, an unexpected illness, or a home repair that has to be done...now! So we say that we just don't have time to sit with the Lord; there are too many responsibilities that must be taken care of.

Aligning Our Priorities

Go back and read that last sentence again. Are we really so focused on this world that we can't find time to spend with the One who created it? Do we really not understand that Jesus is the one thing we need to sustain us in this life? Is God really that low on our list of priorities?

If we're honest, all of us have times in our lives when we would say, "Yes, I haven't had time to spend with God and no, He has not been my top priority." So what can we do to ensure that God is getting not only the time He deserves, but the time He wants to spend with us? How do we find time in this busy life to slow down and just sit at His feet?

First, realize that God should get the firstfruits of your whole life. Proverbs 3:9 says, "Honor the Lord with your wealth, with the firstfruits of all your crops." This verse specifically references giving to the Lord out of our wealth, but we all have a wealth of time, and God should get the first and the best of that as well.

For me, this means waking up early and giving the first portion of my day to Him. I intentionally get up at least an hour before I have to in order to make sure I have time to read the Word, pray, and journal my thoughts to God. Notice the word *intentionally*. I do this on purpose; it is part of my daily schedule, the first thing on my agenda.

With my work and my family, once the morning gets started, there is always somebody who needs something from me. That first hour in the morning is the one time I am alone, nobody needs anything, and I can give my full attention to Bible study and prayer. It's the time I can sit at His feet and listen to what He has to say.

Mornings may not be your best time. Some people are night owls; they feel more capable of focusing late, right before bed. The point is that you need to intentionally, on purpose, find your best time and give it to the Lord—not when it fits into your schedule. If you wait until your schedule slows down, you will never find time. You need to make it part of your schedule, a time that is on your agenda that you are not going to give up, just as important (actually, more important) than keeping an appointment.

We all schedule appointments. We set aside time to take care of our physical health. For example, we see doctors, dentists, optometrists, etc. because it is important to take care of our bodies. How much more important it is to take care of our spiritual health! Make that daily appointment with Jesus, time when you will sit at His feet and listen to Him. Don't allow anything to be so important that you have to cancel that appointment with Him. You have time. Maybe you haven't *made* the time, but you *have* the time. Look today at what needs to be eliminated from your busy life so that God gets your best time.

Mary, Martha, and Us

Get a picture in your mind of Mary sitting at the feet of Jesus. There she sat, knowing full well that the house wasn't ready for company. She wasn't blind to the fact that her sister was bustling about, preparing for their company. While those things were important to her, they paled in comparison to time at her Savior's feet. She understood that the preparations could wait because what Jesus had to teach her was so much more important. Mary found what was better. Let's follow her example and do the same.

Balance Your Mary and Martha

Sit at His Feet

Take some time to sit with the Lord and ask Him if you've been giving Him your firstfruits and your best time. Ask Him to show you what obstacles have been in your way. Are you having a tough time talking with someone you can't see? Are you unsure how to hear His voice? Is there no time to spend with Him because you are filling up so much of your day with activity?

Meditate on the following verses as you sit at His feet:

- Psalm 46:10 – "He says, 'Be still, and know that I am God.'"
- Proverbs 3:5-6 – "Trust in the Lord with all your heart and lean not on your own understanding; in all your ways submit to him, and he will make your paths straight."
- Philippians 4:13 – "I can do all this through him who gives me strength."

Learn from Him

Take some time to think about and journal what you read in this chapter. Use the following questions to guide your thoughts.

- What is your best time of day, your "firstfruits," the time when your mind is the clearest and you can focus best?
- What obstacles get in your way when you try to focus on the Lord and His Word?
- What can you learn from the people in Scripture mentioned in this chapter who were found at the feet of Jesus?

Serve Him

Don't turn another page of this book until you have torn down the obstacles that the Lord revealed to you during your time with Him. Make a divine appointment and commit to sticking to it every day—even when your schedule seems to loom over you. Journal the steps you will take to make and keep your appointment with Jesus.

Put these passages of Scripture into practice as you serve Him:

- James 4:8 – "Come near to God and he will come near to you."
- Proverbs 3:9 – "Honor the Lord with your wealth, with the firstfruits of all your crops."
- John 15:5 – "I am the vine; you are the branches. If you remain in me and I in you, you will bear much fruit; apart from me you can do nothing."

3

Don't Get Distracted

But Martha was distracted by all the preparations that had to be made (Luke 10:40a).

This part of the account of Mary and Martha causes a pang of conviction to enter my heart. So many times I have determined to sit quietly with the Lord and before I know it, I'm looking around the house at all of the things I need to do. The floor needs to be vacuumed, the books on the bookshelf need to be straightened, laundry needs to be washed, the dishwasher needs emptied, and on and on.

Sometimes I read a passage of Scripture, and I decide to sit quietly and meditate on it for a while. Then my thoughts start wandering. I think about things that need to be done at work, or I start thinking about a conversation I had with someone the day before. Whatever it might be, I get distracted.

Life's Distractions

This is exactly what happened to Martha. Notice the first four words of the focus verse for this chapter. "But Martha was distracted." I am certain that Martha knew just as well as Mary who this visitor was that came to see them that day. And in that knowing, I'm sure that she immediately got anxious about the house not being ready for guests; that is where her focus went—she got distracted. All the things that needed to be done took precedence over the presence of Jesus. And if we are honest, we tend to be much more like Martha than like Mary.

Life is so busy, and we are so used to getting what we want quickly. We forget what it means to just sit still and be quiet. We wake up every day with an agenda; a list of to-do's that just have to be accomplished. With the best of intentions, we make the appointment with Jesus that we talked about in the last chapter, but during that time that we've set aside, we are thinking about the schedule for the day.

Or maybe we've set aside the time to intentionally read the Word and sit with Jesus, but we're watching the clock; after all, we've set a certain amount of time, and we can't spend more time than what we've set aside because those items on the daily agenda just can't wait. And you know that the whole world will come crashing down if we don't fulfill everything on that list. (At least that's how it feels to those who, like me, are goal-driven, task-oriented schedulers!)

Let God Be God

Don't get me wrong; I know there are schedules to keep, jobs we need to get to, appointments that can't be cancelled. But if you're finding yourself rushed through your time with Jesus, maybe you've picked the wrong time of day to make that most important appointment.

Remember previously how it was mentioned that you need to give the Lord the first or the best part of your day. If your time with Him is rushed, that can't be the best part you can offer Him. Assess the time that you've set aside. Is there a better time when you won't feel so distracted? Make sure you're offering Him the absolute best time that you have.

Also consider this: maybe it is better to stop having our own agenda and let the Lord determine what will happen with our day.

After all, He is in control of it anyway, not us. Think about Proverbs 16:9, "In their hearts humans plan their course, but the Lord establishes their steps." Or consider James 4:13-17. Specifically, in verse 15, he says, "Instead, you ought to say, 'If it is the Lord's will, we will live and do this or that.'"

It isn't wrong to plan out your day and have an idea of what you want to accomplish. But are you willing to have those plans changed if that is what the Lord thinks is best? Are you able to adjust your plans to match what the Lord has for you each day? Can you let Him interrupt your plans with something He sees as more important? First and foremost, can you spend the necessary time at the feet of Jesus to hear what He wants on that agenda?

Jesus with the Father

Jesus Himself had to take time alone to pray and spend time with His Father. Luke 5:16 says, "But Jesus often withdrew to lonely places and prayed." Let's explore some of those times and then see if we can use those instances as examples for ourselves to draw closer to the Lord in our quiet times. Find ways you can eliminate the distractions of this life and imitate Jesus in your time with the Lord.

One of Jesus' times of prayer is found in Luke 6:12 where it says, "One of those days Jesus went out to a mountainside to pray, and spent the night praying to God." Jesus went off by Himself to pray to the Father, and He prayed all night. According to the verses that follow, the next morning is when He chose the twelve disciples and designated them as apostles.

This indicates to me that the night He spent with the Father was to gain guidance as to which of the disciples would be chosen for His inner circle. Jesus needed wisdom, so He went off by Himself where there would be no distractions and spent the night with His Father. We too can gain wisdom for decisions from the Father when we choose to spend time alone, away from the distractions of the world, talking to Him.

Another time when Jesus was alone with the Father is found in Matthew 14:23. Here it says, "After he had dismissed them, he went up on a mountainside by himself to pray. Later that night, he was there alone." Looking at the passage before this verse, we see that Jesus had just performed the miracle of feeding the large crowd of 5,000 men plus women and children. Just before that, He had withdrawn by Himself on a boat, but the crowds followed Him. "He had compassion on that crowd and healed their sick" (John 14:14), and then He fed them. Even before that, in John 13, we see that Jesus had been traveling about, teaching the people through parables.

We have to remember that Jesus, though fully God, was fully human. This was a busy time. He was doing a lot of work, He was taking care of needy people, and He got tired. So after He fed the 5,000 plus people, He withdrew by Himself to pray. He even told the disciples to get on a boat and go ahead of Him so He would have no distractions whatsoever.

Jesus needed that alone time with the Father to be refreshed and revived. We also need these times of refreshing and recharging. We can grow so weary and tired, and this can discourage us from the important work the Lord wants us doing. Take some time to just sit with the Lord by yourself, with no distractions, and get refreshed.

Yet another time Jesus went alone to be with His Father is found in Mark 1:35 where it says, "Very early in the morning, while it was still dark, Jesus got up, left the house and went off to a solitary place, where he prayed." Once the disciples found Him, they told Him that everyone was looking for Him, but He said, "Let us go somewhere else—to the nearby villages—so I can preach there also. That is why I have come" (Mark 1:38).

This indicates to me that another reason Jesus would get alone with the Father was for guidance and direction.

The disciples wanted Jesus to come and see and heal the crowds where they already were, because everyone was looking for Him. But Jesus, after spending time alone with the Father, decided that they needed to go somewhere else. Notice He said, "That is why I have come." He had asked the Father for guidance as to where to go and to whom to preach, and the Lord directed His steps.

We so often need His direction. We, like the disciples, get our own ideas of where we should go and what we should do. We make the decision and then ask God to bless it. What we need is to get alone with the Father, set aside all of the distractions, even the distractions of our own thoughts, and ask Him what direction He wants us to take.

Remember, in Isaiah 55:8 God says, "For my thoughts are not your thoughts, neither are your ways my ways." Also, remember Proverbs 16:9 from earlier in the chapter that says we may plan our own course, but it is God who determines our steps. We need to stop and listen to God for direction and guidance. Only then can we be in His will, doing what He wants us to do.

In Matthew 26:36-39, we see another powerful time that Jesus went off by Himself to pray. He took three of His disciples with Him to the Garden of Gethsemane and said to them, "My soul is overwhelmed with sorrow to the point of death. Stay here and keep watch with me" (Matthew 26:38). Then He went off by Himself to pray.

Jesus knew that He was about to be arrested, mocked, flogged, and crucified. He was about to go through the greatest physical, mental, and spiritual trial of His life. He was about to take on the sin debt of the entire world. We are told in Luke 22:44 that He was in such anguish that "he prayed more earnestly, and his sweat was like drops of blood falling to the ground."

Alone Time Is Crucial

Clearly, the vital times that Jesus needed to be alone with the Father were in times of trial, hardship, and anguish. He knew that He couldn't do it alone. Without the strength of the Father, He knew that "the spirit is willing, but the flesh is weak" (Matthew 26:41). How perfectly this describes us!

We desire God's will for us, but our flesh is weak in fulfilling it. We go through times of trial and hardship that we can't handle on our own. We need the strength of the Father to make it through those times that are the toughest. Jesus could not endure the burden on His own, and neither can we. We must get alone with the Father and get the strength that only He can provide. Get rid of the distractions and rely on His goodness.

Let's review these four areas where we see Jesus spending time alone with the Father. First, He needed to gain wisdom and guidance. Next, He needed refreshed and renewed after a period of working very hard. Then, He needed direction about where God wanted Him to go. And finally, He needed strength to get through a trial. Remember that everything Jesus did while physically on this earth was an example for us to follow.

I think that this is one of the most important examples that He gave us: get away from any and all distractions and sit alone with your heavenly Father. The four areas where we see Jesus needing the Father are the same areas where we need Him. Jesus couldn't fulfill the mission for which He was sent without God's wisdom, refreshing, direction, and strength, and neither can we.

Believe me, Jesus was a terribly busy man, but He made it a point to take the time to sit at the feet of the Father. He didn't allow the busyness and distractions of this world to get in the way of spending that crucial time with God. There was no way He was going to make it without the help of the Father. If Jesus, the Holy One of God, couldn't get through this life without time spent with God, what makes us think we can?

An Eternal Focus

What it boils down to is this: don't be the seed that fell among the thorns. Let me explain. In Luke chapter 8, Jesus told a parable about different kinds of seeds, but the seed that fell among thorns speaks to those who are distracted. Jesus explains it like this in verse 14: "The seed that fell among thorns stands for those who hear, but as they go on their way they are choked by life's worries, riches and pleasures, and they do not mature."

It is so easy to be distracted by the world around us and lose our focus on Christ. The reality is that this world is where we live. It is what we can see, touch and feel. We need to constantly remind ourselves that this is not our permanent home. We are just passing through, and, if we are in Christ, our eternal home is heaven.

To see some great examples of people who lived with an eternal focus, free from distraction, go to Hebrews 11. Here we see a list of people who, although faced with hardship and uncertainty, kept their lives fixated on eternity, not this world. This chapter recounts Abel, Enoch, Noah, Abraham, Joseph, Moses, and so many more who, by faith, lived out God's call without letting this world distract them. Verses 13-16 sums up perfectly what it looks like to keep your focus in the right place:

All these people were still living by faith when they died. They did not receive the things promised; they only saw them and welcomed them from a distance, admitting that they were foreigners and strangers on earth. People who say such things show that they are looking for a country of their own. If they had been thinking of the country they had left, they would have had opportunity to return. Instead, they were longing for a better country—a heavenly one. Therefore God is not ashamed to be called their God, for he has prepared a city for them.

Like these people of faith, keep yourself focused on your true and eternal home instead of being distracted by the worries of this world.

Jesus taught this same concept when He said to "seek first his kingdom and his righteousness" (Matthew 6:33). Instead of looking around at all of the things on your earthly agenda, look up, and seek His kingdom. When you do that, when you focus on the eternal rather than the temporary, all that Jesus has for you comes into focus.

It is of the utmost importance that you do not let this world distract you from seeing and spending time with Jesus. Nothing in this world can compare to Him. Nothing this world can give you can even hold a candle to the richness and blessing He has to offer. Seek Him first, and don't be distracted.

Mary, Martha, and Us

Take some time to think about what Martha was doing when Jesus came to visit. She was making preparations, making sure that her guest was well cared for. She was tidying up and making food, both of which were important and necessary. It wasn't what she was doing that was the problem. It was the fact that she was distracted by all that needed done. She was so focused on what needed to be done for Jesus that she missed the best thing: spending time with Jesus.

So remember, there are very important works that we need to do for Jesus, but there is never anything that is more important than the time you spend with Him. As a matter of fact, everything you do for Jesus is meaningless when your focus is in the wrong place.

Be sure to sit at His feet first and get His wisdom, refreshing, direction, and strength. He will then show you what it is He wants you doing for Him. Give Him the first and the best part of your day. Don't get so distracted by your own agenda that you miss the very best thing: time with your Savior and best friend.

Lay aside the distractions. Turn off the phone and get in a room without a television to turn on. Forget the schedule for the day. Pick a time when nobody will need anything from you. Just sit at the feet of Jesus for a while and listen to what He has to teach you. Then you will have all you need to serve Him the way He intends.

Balance Your Mary and Martha

Sit at His Feet

Sit quietly with Jesus and allow Him to show you what distracts you. Do you have a habit of turning to electronics every time you have a quiet moment? Maybe your busy schedule doesn't allow for much quiet time. Ask Jesus to reveal these distractions, and be honest about which ones need to be removed.

Meditate on the following verses as you sit at His feet:

- Mark 4:18-19 – "Still others...hear the word; but the worries of this life...come in and choke the word, making it unfruitful."

- Romans 12:2 – "Do not conform to the pattern of this world, but be transformed by the renewing of your mind."

- 1 John 2:15 – "Do not love the world or anything in the world."

Learn from Him

Take some time to think about and journal what you read in this chapter. Use the following questions to guide your thoughts.

- What are some distractions that you notice getting in the way of your time with the Lord?

- What adjustments do you need to make to your thinking or attitude to get to the place where you are comfortable with letting go of your own plans and letting the Lord determine your agenda?

- What lessons did you draw from the moments Jesus went to spend time alone with the Father?

31

Serve Him

Journal some practical ways that you can stop being distracted when you know you should be spending time with the Lord. Determine what your quiet time with Him will look like so that you aren't distracted and you can focus only on Him.

Put these passages of Scripture into practice as you serve Him:

- Hebrews 12:2 – "fixing our eyes on Jesus, the pioneer and perfecter of faith. For the joy set before him he endured the cross, scorning its shame, and sat down at the right hand of the throne of God."

- Colossians 3:2 – "Set your minds on things above, not on earthly things."

- Proverbs 4:25 – "Let your eyes look straight ahead; fix your gaze directly before you."

4

The Need to Serve

But Martha was distracted by all the preparations that had to be made (Luke 10:40a).

Although Martha allowed the distraction of preparing for her guest to get in the way, her heart was in the right place. She had the desire to serve the Lord. She wanted everything to be exactly right for her visitor. Often when studying this account in Scripture, we are so hard on Martha for not stopping and sitting at Jesus' feet like Mary did.

I won't argue that she should have laid aside the distractions and done just that, but I would also like to focus on what Martha did right that day. She didn't neglect serving the Lord. She may have misplaced her priorities, but at least the focus was to serve her Lord and Savior. Mary may have found what was better, but that doesn't mean that what Martha was doing wasn't good.

Instructions on Service

Scripture is clear that we are to serve the Lord and do everything for Him. Here are just a few examples:

- Colossians 3:23-24: "Whatever you do, work at it with all your heart, as working for the Lord, not for human masters, since you know that you will receive an inheritance from the Lord as a reward. It is the Lord Christ you are serving."

- Romans 12:11: "Never be lacking in zeal, but keep your spiritual fervor, serving the Lord."
- John 12:26: "Whoever serves me must follow me; and where I am, my servant also will be. My Father will honor the one who serves me."
- Luke 4:8, "Jesus answered, It is written: 'Worship the Lord your God and serve him only.'"

The instructions from the Lord are clear: we are to be serving Him. So which is it? Should we sit at His feet or serve Him? The answer is both, but we have to find a balance between the two with the aim of not neglecting one so that we can do the other. Service to the Lord cannot be neglected; that is the way in which the Gospel is spread and more people are saved.

Here is the key: if you want a clear answer to the way God wants you to serve Him, you must sit at His feet and listen to what He has to say. He will show you exactly what He wants you doing, and you will find that instruction in your quiet time at His feet. Then you can get up and act out of obedience, serving Him according to what He has revealed to your heart.

James 1:22-25 speaks to this idea. James very clearly to says to "not merely listen to the word, and so deceive yourselves. Do what it says." He compares it to looking in a mirror. Before you leave the house to go out in public, you probably check your appearance in the mirror. How silly it would be if you saw in your reflection that you had food smeared all over your face or your hair was sticking up, and you walked outside and just forgot about it, thinking that you looked just fine?

That's what James says it's like when you hear from God and don't act on it; you are deceiving yourself. Don't lie to yourself that everything is fine if you are sitting quietly with the Lord but then not obeying what He is telling you. Act on what the Lord is telling you to do.

Abram's Example

Let's look at a few people whose stories are recorded in Scripture to get a picture of how listening and serving go hand in hand. First, look at Abram, who would later be called Abraham. In Genesis chapter 12, God told Abram to leave his home country and go to the place that He would show him. Looking at verse 4, we see, "So Abram went, as the Lord had told him." Look at the pattern here. Abram got instructions from the Lord, and he obeyed them. It seems so simple, but think about what had to have happened for this seemingly simple event to occur.

Abram had to hear from God, and to do that, he had to be sitting quietly with Him and listening. Abram didn't even have super clear instructions. God simply said, "Go...to the land that I will show you" (Genesis 12:1), followed by a promise to make him into a great nation. Abram was so in tune with the Lord that he didn't question, he just obeyed. His willingness to quietly listen to God turned into the ability to serve Him and do exactly what He said. He didn't neglect serving the Lord once he heard from Him.

Later, in Genesis 22, after Abram's name had been changed to Abraham and he had his only son Isaac, the son of the Promise, God spoke to him again. This time He asked Abraham to go and sacrifice his son as a burnt offering to the Lord. Again, the first step was for Abraham to hear the voice of God, and he clearly did. When God called his name in Genesis 22:1, Abraham replied, "Here I am." This short phrase has so much significance. When someone said that to the Lord, they meant, "I'm here, Lord. I'm listening."

What a shock it must have been for Abraham to hear this request from God. This was Abraham's son that was given as God's promise, the only one through whom the promise of him becoming the father of many nations could be fulfilled, and he was being asked to sacrifice him. But we see that, starting in Genesis 22:3, Abraham got up early the next morning and was obedient to God. We're not told this in Scripture, but I'm guessing that Abraham had quite the sleepless night sitting quietly before the Lord to get the strength to do this.

And early the next morning, Abraham got up, determined to serve the Lord. You see, he didn't understand completely, but he knew he had heard from God, and now he was going to be obedient to the service that God told him to perform. Here we see ultimate trust in God's plan and purpose.

In Genesis 22:7, during the walk to the place where the offering would occur, Isaac had the following conversation with his father. "The fire and wood are here," Isaac said, "but where is the lamb for the burnt offering?" Abraham replied in verse 8, "God himself will provide the lamb for the burnt offering, my son."

The writer of Hebrews, when recounting this event, said it this way: "Abraham reasoned that God could even raise the dead, and so in a manner of speaking he did receive Isaac back from death" (Hebrews 11:19). So, even though Abraham didn't completely understand how it was going to work out, even though the plan didn't make any sense, he was still obedient and served the Lord in the way that he was called. He didn't neglect serving the Lord. He knew that God had a plan, and he didn't have to understand all of the details in order to be obedient.

Think about how this applies to our lives. In both instances, Abraham didn't understand exactly what God was calling him to do. First, he was told to get up and move to an unknown location, one that God would show him when he got there. Then, he was told to sacrifice his only son who was to make him the father of many nations as was promised.

Sacrificing his son was an act that would certainly make that promise null and void. Abraham knew all along that God is a God who is faithful and keeps His promises. He didn't doubt that God would take care of him and fulfill His plan, even though what he was asked to do didn't seem to make sense.

How did he know all of this? How did he have so much trust? Because he first sat at the feet of God and listened to what He had to say. That's where he gained the strength and the trust to serve Him. And while sitting at His feet was so important, service had to follow. He had to be obedient to what he learned during those quiet times. He didn't neglect serving the Lord.

We too must follow what we learned in the previous two chapters in this book: sit at His feet with no distractions and listen to what He has to say. Then the next step is action. Get up and do what it is the Lord told you to do. Recall the passage from James 1 above. God speaks to us through His Word. Spending quiet time in the Word is a great way to hear what the Lord has to say to you. But if you only do that—just listen—it hasn't done you any good. You have to take the next step and do what the Lord has told you to do. Don't neglect serving Him.

Ananias' Example

The account of another man in Scripture who heard the Lord and acted in obedience is found in Acts chapter 9. Saul (who would become the apostle Paul) had just met Jesus on his way to Damascus, where he was going to persecute Christians. Saul's main occupation at the time was hunting down Christians and throwing them in prison or approving of their death because of their faith.

When Jesus miraculously appeared to him on the road to Damascus, Saul believed in Jesus, but he was struck blind in the process. There was a man in Damascus named Ananias who would have had no idea that any of this took place. He did know, as did all believers, who Saul was, and that he was bad news for Christians.

But there Ananias was, sitting quietly in his home, when the Lord spoke to him. God gave Ananias specific, detailed directions of where to go to find Saul and restore his sight. Ananias told the Lord that he knew why Saul had come to Damascus: to throw people like him in prison.

But the Lord told him to go because He had chosen Saul to be a witness to the Gentiles. So Ananias was obedient. He took what the Lord had said to him and turned it into action. He didn't neglect serving the Lord, even though he was afraid of Saul because he knew he had the power and authority to do him harm.

Moses' Example

An additional example can be found in Scripture of someone who heard from God but was afraid to be obedient to serve Him. In Exodus 3 and 4, we see a progression of excuses that Moses gave to God, all of the reasons that he couldn't serve the way he was being called. After being told by God to go to Pharaoh and demand that he let the Israelites go, Moses was afraid.

Listen to some of what Moses said to God in response to His call. In Exodus 3:11, Moses said, "Who am I that I should go to Pharaoh and bring the Israelites out of Egypt?" Later, in Exodus 3:13, he said, "Suppose I go to the Israelites and say to them, 'The God of your fathers has sent me to you,' and they ask me, 'What is his name?' Then what shall I tell them?"

Moses also said, in Exodus 4:1, "What if they do not believe me or listen to me and say, 'The Lord did not appear to you?'" Finally, Moses said to God in Exodus 4:10, "Pardon your servant, Lord. I have never been eloquent, neither in the past nor since you have spoken to your servant. I am slow of speech and tongue."

Just listen to these excuses. I'm not good enough. I don't know what to say. They won't believe me. I'm not a good speaker. And notice how every excuse is an excuse of fear—fear of not being able to complete the task God had laid in front of him. Every excuse offered up had to do with his own abilities or lack thereof. He forgot to listen to the answers God was giving him about being with him and giving him the strength he needed.

At the end of this conversation with God, in Exodus 4:13, Moses finally said, "Pardon your servant, Lord. Please send someone else." Moses was so afraid that he tried to get God to just send someone else to do the mighty work that God wanted him doing. He almost missed out on the amazing journey that God wanted to put him on because of fear. He almost neglected serving the Lord.

Paralyzing Fear

How often we allow our fear to stop us from serving the Lord. Our fear, like Ananias, may be that we will be persecuted for our faith. Maybe we're not afraid of being thrown in prison or killed, but we are afraid of being ridiculed by those who don't believe what we believe. Or maybe, like Moses, we have a fear of failure, a fear that we are not good enough to perform the task in front of us. Sometimes we are afraid to serve because it will mean making a big change in our lives that we just don't feel ready to make.

In any case, fear holds us back from serving God. That fear comes straight from the devil. 2 Timothy 1:7 tells us, "For the Spirit God gave us does not make us timid, but gives us power, love and self-discipline." If God calls us to a task, He will give us the power to fulfill that task. Likewise, Isaiah 41:10 says, "So do not fear, for I am with you; do not be dismayed, for I am your God. I will strengthen you and help you; I will uphold you with my righteous right hand." You have no need to fear when you are acting in obedience to something God has called you to do.

I confess that I tend to be more like Moses and Ananias than Abraham. I distinctly remember a time when I did exactly what Moses did and made excuses for not stepping out in faith. It was my third year of teaching, and for those three years, I had taught fifth grade. It had become my passion, what I felt was my niche.

I loved the age group of kids who were too old to be treated like kids but too young to be treated as adults. Then the school board where I was working asked me to make a move. Part of my degree was in mathematics, and they wanted me to move up to the middle school level and help strengthen the math program.

What was my first response—my knee-jerk reaction? No way. There was no way I was going to teach teenagers. They had way too much attitude. I wasn't prepared for the more rigorous curriculum; that age group just wasn't for me.

Any excuse I could make, I made. Over the course of the next week or two, I heard two sermons on the radio, one particular song several times, and a sermon at church—all on stepping out of the boat. God gave me a message loud and clear that He wanted me to get out of my comfort zone. I still didn't want to, but I decided to try it.

I realized that I was responding out of fear and had forgotten the promises that God had made. It was only when I remembered to sit at His feet and learn from His Word that I was able to go forth boldly and act out of obedience. And the result? I have now been teaching middle and high school math for eighteen years, and they have been the best years of my career.

I have been blessed to take two groups of teens to a youth conference and watch them learn and grow in the Lord. God knew the plan He had for me was the right one, and had I not been obedient, I would have missed one of the biggest blessings He had to offer. It was only the combination of sitting at His feet and serving Him that brought that blessing to fruition.

Mary, Martha, and Us

Let's now get back to Mary and Martha. Remember, Martha was serving while Mary was sitting at the Lord's feet and listening to Him. What we need to realize is that both women were doing the right thing. Mary only found what was better because she didn't allow herself to be distracted; she understood that learning from Jesus had to come before serving Him.

Martha understood how important it was to serve Jesus, she just got her priorities mixed up and failed to understand that sitting quietly and listening had to come before action. But she did understand that she shouldn't neglect serving the Lord.

Let's be sure to recognize this in our own lives. There has to be a time that we sit quietly with the Lord and receive instruction and encouragement from Him. There also has to be a time when we put that instruction into action and serve Him. That's what we are called to do.

Be sure not to neglect either one of these things. Sit at His feet, bask in His goodness, and receive the instruction that He wants to give you. Then take that instruction and live it out in humble service to Him. Let Him speak to your heart, and let yourself respond lovingly by serving Him with your whole being. You will be extremely blessed when you do.

Balance Your Mary and Martha

Sit at His Feet

Use some of your quiet time with the Lord to ask Him where He wants you to serve Him. Is there a ministry He is asking you to take on? Is there a change He wants you to make so that you can serve Him in an area you've never served before? Have a conversation with the Lord and ask Him to show you where and how He wants you serving Him.

Meditate on the following verses as you sit at His feet:

- James 1:22 – "Do not merely listen to the word, and so deceive yourselves. Do what it says."

- Deuteronomy 13:4 – "It is the Lord your God you must follow, and him you must revere. Keep his commands and obey him; serve him and hold fast to him."

- Joshua 22:5 – "But be very careful...to serve him with all your heart."

Learn from Him

Take some time to think about and journal what you read in this chapter. Use the following questions to guide your thoughts.

- What did you learn in this chapter about the balance of sitting at Jesus' feet and serving Him?

- What encouragement can you gain from the experiences of Abraham, Ananias, and Moses in listening to God and obeying Him?

- How can you overcome your fears, step out of your comfort zone, and serve the Lord in the way He is calling you?

Serve Him

Figure out what might be holding you back from service. Is it that you haven't spent the time listening to Him, and you're unsure where or how to serve? Is it that you are afraid in some way to step out in the service He's calling you to? Give those obstacles to Him and allow Him to lead you and strengthen you. Then step out in faith and do what He's called you to do. Record in your journal the steps you need to take to move into the service he's called you to.

Put these passages of Scripture into practice as you serve Him:

- Colossians 2:6 – "So then, just as you received Christ Jesus as Lord, continue to live your lives in him."

- Ephesians 6:7 – "Serve wholeheartedly, as if you were serving the Lord, not people."

- Luke 6:38 – "Give, and it will be given to you. A good measure, pressed down, shaken together and running over, will be poured into your lap. For with the measure you use, it will be measured to you."

5

Lord, Don't You Care?

She came to him and asked, "Lord, don't you care that my sister has left me to do the work by myself? Tell her to help me!" (Luke 10:40b)

This next verse in the account of Mary and Martha reveals so much about our hearts. We can fall into two very unhealthy thought patterns when we serve. First, we start to feel like we are working so hard for nothing, and God doesn't see or care. Then we start to notice others who aren't serving the way we think they should, and we become resentful.

If we let these thought patterns grab hold of us, we lash out at God and others, demanding that they help us in our area of service. These inclinations need to be addressed, and so we will take the time to break each of them down and learn how to avoid them. This chapter is dedicated to the first one: thinking that God doesn't see or care what we are doing. This is a symptom of spiritual burnout, something we need to be very careful to avoid.

Remember, Martha's problem wasn't that she was serving the Lord instead of sitting at His feet; her problem was that she became distracted with serving. She started to feel overwhelmed when she looked around at all the preparations that still needed to be made.

When she looked over at her sister sitting at Jesus' feet, and Jesus teaching her, she felt like she was doing all of that work for nothing. Or perhaps she knew that Mary had found what was better, but she thought the preparations had to come first. In any case, she felt unappreciated, or at least underappreciated. So she asked Jesus, "Lord don't you care?"

Spiritual Burn-Out

This is so often what happens in our own lives. We want to serve the Lord, and we feel called to do it in a certain way. We pour our hearts and souls into the ministry area that we feel led into, and we work hard to see that the ministry is a success.

Then we reach a point where it feels like we're stuck. We begin to feel as if the things we are doing are not effective. We get frustrated. Then we start to question whether God really did call us into that area of ministry after all. We don't see the results of our labor, the fruit of our work, and so we ask God, "Lord, don't you care? Can't you see how hard I'm working? Is all of this work really worth it?"

There have been times in my life when I've felt this way. I have worked in Christian education for more than twenty years. I have always felt called to work in this field, and I know that God has given me the gift of teaching. Teaching in Christian education, however, especially in the area where I live, does not pay as well as teaching in the public school arena. I have always been willing to make that sacrifice, but there were times when that meant that my budget was tight, and I had a tough time making ends meet.

A few times over the years when I found myself balancing my checking account and I was unable get all the bills paid, that I said to God, "Don't you care? You called me into this line of work, I know this is where You want me to be, so why is this so difficult?" God answered me every time, providing for me in ways that I never expected, but in the moment, I felt like God had forgotten about me. I would get stuck thinking that He didn't care.

At times I also found myself in this struggle working with students. When I poured my heart and soul into teaching my students the truth of God's Word, their behavior seemingly reflected that I had taught them nothing. I would be tempted to think, *Is this really what I'm supposed to be doing? Is anything I'm teaching these students sinking in?* Again, God has provided encouragement to me in the form of students coming back to visit after they graduated to thank me for being faithful to teach them. I also know that some of my rewards will come to me in heaven, and I will see all the fruits of my labor there. But again, in the moment, it can be frustrating and seem like God is silent or doesn't care.

Before we go any further and explore people in Scripture who felt this way, let me encourage you with 1 Corinthians 15:58:

> *Therefore, my dear brothers and sisters, stand firm. Let nothing move you. Always give yourselves fully to the work of the Lord, because you know that your labor in the Lord is not in vain.*

Your service to God is never worthless. Nothing you do for the Lord goes unseen or gets ignored. God cares about all of it, even when you don't feel it. When you start to feel like your service is all for nothing, go back to this verse and meditate on it; sit at His feet with it. Stand firm. Do not be moved. God does indeed care.

Elijah's Example

When you feel defeated in your service to God, you are not alone. One example of a person in Scripture who felt this way was Elijah. In 1 Kings 19, he was sitting under a broom tree asking the Lord to take his life. God had just shown him a great victory in chapter 18, destroying the name of the false god Baal and ridding the land of his false prophets. But because of that, Elijah's own life was being threatened, and he was at the point of giving up.

Elijah said to God,

I have been very zealous for the Lord God Almighty. The Israelites have rejected your covenant, torn down your altars, and put your prophets to death with the sword. I am the only one left, and now they are trying to kill me too (1 Kings 19:10).

Here is my modern day paraphrase: "I have worked so hard for you, Lord. You just helped me to prove that this god Baal is a false god, but the people still reject you, and they want me dead too. Has all of my work been worth it? Don't you care, God?"

I love the way God answered Elijah in verse 11: "Go out and stand on the mountain in the presence of the Lord, for the Lord is about to pass by." Again, my modern day summary, "I know you feel defeated, Elijah, but your labor has not been in vain. Here, let me show myself to you." And then God proceeded to send a powerful wind, an earthquake, and a fire, but God was not in any of those. No, it was in the last thing— the gentle whisper—where Elijah found God.

Elijah repeated his complaint to the Lord, and God encouraged his heart in verses 15 through 18, telling him how his problem would be resolved and that there was, indeed, a remnant that had not bowed down to Baal. Elijah could trust that his labor was not in vain, and that God did care very deeply about him and his service.

Job's Example

Also consider Job. Here was a man who was described as "blameless and upright; he feared God and shunned evil" (Job

1:1). But the Lord allowed Satan in, and he took everything. Job lost his livelihood, his family, and his health. And while he maintained his integrity towards God through all of it, we can see throughout the book of Job that he did question if God cared.

Look in particular at chapter 10. In verse 3, Job said, "Does it please you to oppress me, to spurn the work of your hands, while you smile on the plans of the wicked?" In verse 18, he cried out, "Why then did you bring me out of the womb? I wish I had died before any eye saw me." Can you hear the anguish in Job's voice, wondering what the purpose was of even being born; wondering if God saw and cared about the fact that he had been faithful to Him all of his life?

God had so much to teach Job during this time. Read the end of the book, starting in chapter 38 to see everything God had to say to Job, but it came down to this: of course God cared. He cared enough that he allowed Job to go through terrible suffering so that he could understand that God is sovereign in all things. He wanted Job to learn that God gives and takes away, but His plans are always best, even when our circumstances are not good.

It seems as though, even with Job being called upright and blameless, he still had some growing and maturing to do, and God loved him too much to leave him where he was. After Job learned these lessons, God doubly restored everything Job had lost. He didn't leave him in despair; He cared about him too much to do that. God does care, and He does answer, but He does it in His time and in His way, which is always better than ours.

Jeremiah's Example

Finally, look at the struggles of the prophet Jeremiah. In Jeremiah 20:7-18, it is evident that he was feeling very discouraged. He had spent many years speaking the words that the Lord brought to him, and he had faced ridicule and mocking from those he spoke to. In verse 8, he said, "the word of the Lord has brought me insult and reproach all day long."

You can see Jeremiah's frustration and grief throughout this passage. This complaint sounds so much like the title of this chapter, "Lord, don't You care?" Here was someone who had worked diligently for the Lord and had dedicated his whole life to speaking God's truth, but he couldn't see the fruits of his labor. Instead, all he saw was defeat. He was experiencing spiritual burnout.

Later, however, in chapter 29, Jeremiah had a message for the surviving exiles who were still in Babylon. This was a message of encouragement, a promise to God's people that they would not be in exile forever but would be saved. In this passage, we find one of the most encouraging sentences in Scripture: "For I know the plans I have for you," declares the Lord, "plans to prosper you and not to harm you, plans to give you hope and a future" (Jeremiah 29:11). While Jeremiah was speaking these words to the Israelite exiles, I can't help but think that God was encouraging Jeremiah's own heart at the same time. Just listen to the words of the entire passage of Jeremiah 29:11-14:

> *"For I know the plans I have for you," declares the Lord, "plans to prosper you and not to harm you, plans to give you hope and a future. Then you will call on me and come and pray to me, and I will listen to you. You will seek me and find me when you seek me with all your heart. I will be found by you," declares the Lord, "and will bring you back from captivity. I will gather you from all the nations and places where I have banished you," declares the Lord, "and will bring you back to the place from which I carried you into exile.*

What beautiful words these are! And while the exiles needed to hear this encouraging promise from God, so did Jeremiah, and so do we. When we are going through times where we feel like God doesn't see or care about our service to Him, we can lean on this promise that His plans are for our good, to make us prosperous. We can be sure that we will find Him when we seek Him with all our hearts. And He will bring us back from that place where we feel so far from Him.

Mary, Martha, and Us

Let's look back at what was happening with Mary and Martha. Martha had found herself in this place of spiritual burnout. Her gift was definitely in the area of service, but at this moment, with all that needed done, she was feeling defeated and frustrated.

Her reaction of saying, "Don't You care, Lord" was a symptom that her focus had gotten skewed, and she was looking at the work that needed to be done instead of looking to the Lord. It was through this experience that she learned one of the greatest lessons of her life: it is important to use your spiritual gifts, but it is more important to seek the Lord. Without the latter, the former becomes a burden, not a joy.

Here is the beautiful thing: Jesus will teach us this same lesson and then continue to allow us to use our gifts for His glory. You see, Jesus didn't try to change who Martha was through all of this. Her gift was service, and once she got her priorities adjusted, she continued to use this precious gift.

Look at John 12:1-3. During a second visit to Mary and Martha's house, after Jesus raised their brother Lazarus from the dead, the women again provided dinner for Jesus in their home. Pay close attention to verses 2 and 3. Martha served while Mary anointed Jesus' feet with perfume and wiped them with her hair. This is almost exactly what happened during Jesus' first visit to their house: Martha served, and Mary sat at the feet of Jesus.

This time, though, there was no strife or indication that

Martha was upset with Mary for not helping her serve. It seems that she learned the lesson that her service was important, that Jesus did care about what she was doing. She came to understand that not all acts of service look the same.

We will explore this idea in the chapters to come. For now, realize that Martha was content in her service to the Lord because she learned that He does care about each person's service, no matter how small, and no matter how it compares to the service of others.

Remember this lesson when you are feeling the effects of spiritual burnout. It seems as if we put Christian service on a scale, as if some acts or deeds are better or more spiritual than others. We tend to think that if we are in the nursery watching babies, that isn't near as important as teaching Sunday school. Or if we are serving snacks at VBS, that couldn't be as important as teaching the children the Bible lesson.

In those cases, we are forgetting that Jesus doesn't see acts of service that way. Instead, remember, if you were not in the nursery watching that baby there would be a mother who would be unable to attend Sunday school and receive important teaching. If you weren't serving the snack, maybe the kids would be too focused on their growling tummies to focus on the Bible lesson. The point is, all acts of service matter to God. If you are working for Him, He cares about what you are doing.

That is lesson number one from this chapter's focus verse: God cares about every act of service. Watch for these symptoms of spiritual burnout in your life, subtle indications of frustration, thinking that God doesn't see or care what you are doing. At the beginning of this chapter, I also mentioned another unhealthy thought pattern that gets in the way of our spiritual growth—that people aren't serving the way we think they should. Let's spend some time in the next chapter digging into this and learning how to avoid it.

Balance Your Mary and Martha

Sit at His Feet

Ask Jesus to reveal areas in your life where you feel burnt out. Have you been in the same job or ministry position for many years, and you don't feel as effective as you once did? Does it seem like others get time to rest and you don't? Do you find yourself wondering if Jesus sees or cares about what you do for Him? Let Him speak to your heart and reveal these areas.

Meditate on the following verses as you sit at His feet:

- Psalm 128:2 – "You will eat the fruit of your labor; blessings and prosperity will be yours."

- Psalm 90:17 – "May the favor of the Lord our God…establish the work of our hands."

- Romans 12:11 – "Never be lacking in zeal, but keep your spiritual fervor."

Learn from Him

Take some time to think about and journal what you read in this chapter. Use the following questions to guide your thoughts.

- What can you learn from God's answer to Elijah in the midst of his frustration?

- Consider Job and all of the suffering he went through. What can you do to grasp the concept that God is sovereign and His plans are always better, even when your circumstances aren't good?

- Look again at Jeremiah 29:11-14. What encouragement do you gain from these words, knowing that the Lord sees, cares, and will make your way prosperous in His time and His way? What do you need to do to let go of your own plans and give them over to God?

Serve Him

Recognize that while sometimes this feeling of burnout means that you need a change, it isn't always the case. Take a long, prayerful look at the ways you serve the Lord and see if change is needed or if you just need some encouragement to persevere right where you are. Once you hear from Him clearly, let Him spur you on to action. Allow Him to be your encourager, knowing that He truly does care about your service to Him.

Put these passages of Scripture into practice as you serve Him:

- Proverbs 16:3 – "Commit to the Lord whatever you do, and he will establish your plans."
- Ecclesiastes 3:22 – "So I saw that there is nothing better for a person than to enjoy their work, because that is their lot. For who can bring them to see what will happen after them?"
- Colossians 3:23 – "Whatever you do, work at it with all your heart, as working for the Lord, not for human masters."

6

They Aren't Working!

She came to him and asked, "Lord, don't you care that my sister has left me to do the work by myself? Tell her to help me!" (Luke 10:40b)

After Martha said to Jesus, "Don't you care?" she proceeded to complain that she was left to do the work all by herself while her sister just sat there. Oh, how prone we are to act the same way. Sometimes when we are serving the Lord, and we are involved in a ministry that we know is important, we tend to notice the people who aren't as busy as we are—or so we think.

We are creatures who get so laser focused on our own lives and work that we think if we don't see someone as busy as we are, they must not be working. When we think this way, we are forgetting two things: we need to mind our own business, and just because you don't see someone working doesn't mean they aren't.

Let's begin with the idea of minding our own business. Paul was pretty clear in 1 Thessalonians 4:11, when he said, "and to make it your ambition to lead a quiet life: You should mind your own business and work with your hands, just as we told you." It doesn't get much more straightforward than that. Lead a quiet life, mind your own business, and find some work to do. It is not your job to worry about what everyone else is doing. You are only responsible for you.

The Problem of Pride

Consider pride as the root cause of worrying about what others are doing instead of focusing on the work that the Lord gave you. We all have an innate tendency to compare ourselves to others. If we can see that we are working harder, or our work is more important or more effective, it makes us feel better. Pride takes our focus off of the Lord and onto ourselves.

To some who were confident of their own righteousness and looked down on everyone else, Jesus told this parable in Luke 18:9-14:

> *Two men went up to the temple to pray, one a Pharisee and the other a tax collector. The Pharisee stood by himself and prayed: "God, I thank you that I am not like other people— robbers, evildoers, adulterers—or even like this tax collector. I fast twice a week and give a tenth of all I get."*

> *But the tax collector stood at a distance. He would not even look up to heaven, but beat his breast and said, "God, have mercy on me, a sinner." I tell you that this man, rather than the other, went home justified before God. For all those who exalt themselves will be humbled, and those who humble themselves will be exalted.*

In this parable, we see two characters: a Pharisee and a tax collector. The people hearing this parable would have understood right away that the Pharisee was the righteous one and the tax collector was the despised one. Listen to the words of the Pharisee in verses 11 and 12:

The Pharisee stood by himself and prayed: "God, I thank you that I am not like other people—robbers, evildoers, adulterers— or even like this tax collector. I fast twice a week and give a tenth of all I get."

His prayer was all about himself—look what I am doing,

God; other people aren't working as hard as I am for you. Pride will cause us to think this way. Instead of focusing on the Lord and thanking Him for the privilege of serving, pride has us focus on ourselves and compare ourselves to others to get our commendation.

Contrast what the Pharisee said with what the tax collector said in verse 13: "But the tax collector stood at a distance. He would not even look up to heaven, but beat his breast and said, 'God, have mercy on me, a sinner.'" One singular focus: his relationship to God. He was not looking around at what others were doing, nor comparing his work to the work of others. Instead, he displayed only humility and a desire to be right with the Lord. The only "me" part of his prayer was to plead with God for mercy and admit before the Lord that he was a sinner. And notice what Jesus said about him in verse 14: "I tell you that this man, rather than the other, went home justified before God."

To eliminate this problem of pride, we need to fully grasp that we are not justified by our works, and God does not sit in heaven comparing our work to somebody else's to see who is more worthy of His mercy and grace. In the parable above, Jesus ends the story with this statement: "For all those who exalt themselves will be humbled, and those who humble themselves will be exalted."

Also, in Ephesians 2:8-9, we're told, "For it is by grace you have been saved, through faith—and this is not from yourselves, it is the gift of God—not by works, so that no one can boast." If God does not look at our works as the means by which we are justified, then why do we? And notice why we are not justified by works: so that no one can boast. God wants to eliminate pride. We need to understand that our salvation comes through Christ alone, and nothing we do could ever earn our way into eternal life with Him.

If our works do not justify us, does that mean that our service to the Lord is not important? Of course not! Remember the last chapter; God sees your service to Him, and He cares deeply about it. But when we start to compare what we are doing to what others are doing, we start to get this prideful idea that we somehow have earned more of God's favor than other people.

Pride creeps into our thinking, and then our service becomes a way of justifying ourselves, not serving the Lord. This is a danger zone. When our service to God becomes about *us* and not about *His kingdom*, it becomes worthless. We need to have an eternal focus, worrying only about how our service builds up the kingdom, not worrying about what others are doing or not doing.

The Problem of Jealousy

Sometimes not minding our own business and comparing what we are doing to what others are doing can lead to just the opposite of pride. We can become discouraged, thinking that others are so much better than we are, and we give up on our service to the Lord. Then, because we are focused on others' work instead of our own, we fall into the danger of talking about and criticizing others. We can see that this happened in Thessalonica. Paul wrote, in 2 Thessalonians 3:11, "We hear that some among you are idle and disruptive. They are not busy; they are busybodies."

When all you can think about is what others are doing and you're not focusing on how you need to grow in your spiritual maturity and service, you can very easily become a "busybody." Many times this comes from a heart of jealousy. It is a spiral of unhealthy thinking.

When we think other people are better at ministry activities than we are, we can become jealous. So, to make ourselves feel better, we criticize their work. Instead, we need to find an area in which we are gifted and use that gift for building up God's kingdom.

I have fallen into this second dangerous way of thinking. I have had a bad habit of comparing my children with those of other families. Social media certainly hasn't helped my self-confidence in this area. When I see pictures of the "perfect" parents and their kids, I get a feeling of not being a good enough mother myself.

I actually hate the professional photographs of families walking in a field hand-in-hand because I know that no family actually does that—no one could be that perfect. I have found myself feeling pangs of jealousy, even after reminding myself that nobody is perfect and that people only post the good and happy moments. (Disclaimer: if you've gotten those beautiful family portraits, don't feel guilty. My feelings about those are just a byproduct of my own insecurities.)

Thankfully, God has shown me that any mistakes I have made in parenting have been redeemed by His blood. He has given me the encouragement that I need to be happy with my family just the way it is and the knowledge that, because I have raised my children in Him, I have done well. I am content with the fact that, although I have never been perfect and I've made mistakes with my kids, I have no reason to compare myself to others.

Even when my children make imperfect decisions, it is not a reason to beat myself up and blame myself. Jesus can redeem all of it. I still find myself looking at young families and thinking, "If only I'd have done that when my kids were small..." It's in those moments that I deliberately stop and remember that God does not call me to compare myself to others. He calls me to take care of my own relationship with Him and let Him do the work.

Unseen Works

Let's look at the second point to remember when you are tempted to say, "Lord, they aren't working for you." Just because you don't see someone working for the Lord doesn't mean they aren't. I understand how frustrating it is when you work so hard in a ministry and you look around and see all of those people who aren't doing anything, who seem to be getting fed and lifted up, but they aren't doing the feeding or uplifting work.

I know that getting people involved in ministry is important, and that it is discouraging when people turn down opportunities to serve. And I know that sometimes people make lame excuses for why they can't serve in a particular area. So remember first that you are only responsible for you. You are the only person for whom you will have to give an account when you see Jesus face to face. But also remember that those people who don't seem to be doing anything for the Lord just might be serving in an area that you don't see.

Consider how many great prayer warriors might be sitting in the pews of the church. You may not see these people actively getting involved in the areas that we traditionally call ministries. They may not teach Sunday school, serve food at church banquets, or help out at vacation Bible school. But their ministry is behind the scenes, praying for the people who are actively involved in these types of activities.

And, oh how important that ministry is! All of the activities and ministry areas of the church have to be led and blessed by the Holy Spirit, and without prayer, we are defeated before we start. So don't count out those who seem idle but are not. Thank the Lord for those who uphold the church's ministry in prayer. They are indispensable.

A Proper Response

Now I am not so naive as to think that everyone who is not actively serving with their hands is actively praying for those who are. The reality is that there are people in the church who simply are not serving the Lord. There are people who will make up any excuse at all to not have to take time out of their busy lives to work for the Lord. Many are content to sit back and be fed but not help feed.

When I say to mind your own business, I don't mean that we don't notice these people. But we need to check our attitude towards them. They are part of the body too, so how can we build them up and "spur them on toward love and good deeds" (Hebrews 10:24)? What can we do to encourage these people and show them that the Lord expects all of us to serve Him, not just sit back and be served?

We can see how Martha's response to her sister not helping could have been handled differently. Instead of getting upset and having the attitude that Mary was just sitting around doing nothing while she did all the work, Martha could have sat down and had a conversation about what was bothering her. If she would have done that, she would have saved herself a lot of frustration.

I'm guessing Jesus would have shown Martha at that moment just what He ended up showing her at the end, that serving Him is good, but getting nourishment and teaching from Him is better. She could have gotten the rest that comes from sitting at the feet of Jesus, and then she and Mary could have served together.

The effective way of drawing people into ministry is being honest, talking to each other in love, and building each other up. When all we do is get frustrated with each other, we alienate ourselves from each other, and then none of our ministry is effective.

How much better it is to lift each other up, talk to each other about what is bothering us, and then serve together. We don't have to be serving in the same way to serve together. Each person's service works in tandem with everyone else's so that the entire body of Christ is built up. God designed His body so that we would all have a part and each part would be important for building up the whole body.

Paul's Teaching

Paul had so much to say about this in 1 Corinthians 12. Before reading on in this chapter, take a moment to open your Bible and read this passage and think about how each person's work is equally as important as that of others. Contemplate how your acts of service fit into the bigger picture.

Let's break down what he had to say to the believers in Corinth about this very important topic. First, in verses 1-11, he says that God distributes spiritual gifts to all believers, and although not all of those gifts are the same, they are given by the same Spirit. These gifts are given for the common good; they are meant to be used to make the body of Christ strong and healthy. Paul goes on in verses 12-27 to compare the body of Christ to our physical bodies. He explains that each part has its place and that each job is just as important as another.

By saying that a foot should not wish it was a hand and an ear should not wish it was an eye, he is telling us that we should not think that our acts of service are more or less important than anybody else's. We should work diligently in any area God has placed us in and rejoice that He gave us that gift. We have no reason to look at what others are doing and compare ourselves to them. Their gift is not our gift, and the body of Christ would not be fully healthy without all of its parts functioning in the way they were designed.

Think a little bit more about this comparison of the body of Christ and our physical bodies. Think about how small your pinky toe is on each foot. How much do you think about your pinky toe as you walk around and do your daily tasks? Probably not very much. But how much do you think about that toe when you stub it on the leg of a chair? It's all you can think about. And did you know that your pinky toe is one of the most important parts of the body for keeping your balance? Without it, you would have to concentrate much harder to stand and to walk without falling.

That is exactly what Paul was getting at. Some acts of service to God aren't noticed as much as others. But when those acts are not fulfilled, when nobody is doing that job, it is noticed in a big way. And as it was stated earlier, just because you don't see somebody's service for the Lord, it doesn't mean they aren't working.

Mary, Martha, and Us

So take this lesson from Martha: your service to the Lord is important. There may be others around you who are not helping you with the work that you are doing, and it may be frustrating you. Don't allow that frustration to cause you to look down on others and get discouraged.

Instead, realize that there may be ways in which those people are working and you just don't see it. If it continues to bother you, don't complain about them; instead, go to them and talk about ministry as you each see it. Ask the Lord for wisdom in how you can serve His body and build up the church.

In these last two chapters, we've looked at two unhealthy ways of thinking that can discourage us: thinking that God doesn't care and feeling like we are doing His work by ourselves. In the next chapter, we will look at what these ways of thinking can lead to: lashing out at others or God out of frustration. Let's learn these lessons together so we can avoid them and keep our spiritual health and the health of the Body of Christ intact.

Balance Your Mary and Martha

Sit at His Feet

Take some time to be honest with yourself and God, admitting the ways in which you have been frustrated with others instead of focusing on how you can serve the Lord. Confess to God instances that you have felt jealousy toward someone else's service. Also tell Him any ways in which you have been prideful, thinking that you are serving more than someone else.

Meditate on the following verses as you sit at His feet:

- Colossians 3:12 – "Clothe yourselves with compassion, kindness, humility, gentleness and patience."

- Romans 15:1 – "Bear with the failings of the weak and not to please ourselves."

- Philippians 2:3 – "Do nothing out of selfish ambition or vain conceit. Rather, in humility value others above yourselves."

Learn from Him

Take some time to think about and journal what you read in this chapter. Use the following questions to guide your thoughts.

- Have you ever found yourself succumbing to the two unhealthy thought patterns described in this chapter—pride or jealousy? What caused those thoughts and feelings?

- How can you find the balance between minding your own business and spurring others on to work for the Lord?

- What is the best way to resolve conflict when it seems as if a person isn't serving the Lord?

Serve Him

Discover what your spiritual gifts are and use them to the best of your ability to glorify God. Find a godly mentor who can help you discover your gifts if you're unsure what they are. Ask the pastor or elders in your church where your service is needed and fill in any gaps in ministry that your church is experiencing. Determine to build up the body of Christ by your acts of service.

Put these passages of Scripture into practice as you serve Him:

- 1 Corinthians 12:1-11 – "There are different kinds of gifts, but the same Spirit distributes them." (v. 4)

- 1 Corinthians 14:12 – "Since you are eager for gifts of the Spirit, try to excel in those that build up the church."

- 1 Timothy 4:14 – "Do not neglect your gift, which was given you through prophecy when the body of elders laid their hands on you."

7

Tell Them to Serve!

She came to him and asked, "Lord, don't you care that my sister has left me to do the work by myself? Tell her to help me!" (Luke 10:40b)

Here is the last thing Martha said in her complaint to Jesus: "Tell her to help me!" Remember from the last chapter that there are those who simply are not serving the Lord, those who are content to be fed but not to feed others. These people can be frustrating, especially for those who work wholeheartedly.

The exclamation point at the end of Martha's request indicates that she was definitely frustrated with her sister. It is in our very nature to point these people out to God and say, "God, tell them to serve You. Why should they just be able to sit there while the rest of Your body does all of the work?" But maybe we can find a better way to handle these feelings.

Check Your Attitude

Let's first look at what Martha did right: she took her complaint to Jesus. When we are frustrated, especially with someone in our family of believers, we should go to Jesus first. What Martha got wrong, however, was that she asked, or rather demanded, that Jesus work out the problem her way.

Instead of going to Jesus with an open heart and mind, she went with her own ideas of how things should be. She went to

Him with a demand instead of a soft heart that would allow her to see that maybe her sister's behavior wasn't the problem. It was her perception of Mary's behavior that caused Martha to complain.

I have to admit that I am prone to talk to Jesus in the same way that Martha did, especially when I know that someone has a gift or talent and they simply aren't using it. I get frustrated. I've caught myself praying words such as, "God, just make them..." or "Father, make them see that...." In those moments, I am basically telling God that I have it all figured out and that He just needs to act to make it happen.

How backwards is that? Instead, the prayer should be, "Lord, soften my heart. Help me to see with your eyes. Why is it that it seems to me that this person isn't serving you? Is there a need in her life that isn't being met? Does she need help finding her gifts and talents so she can better use them for you? Show me what I can do to encourage her heart." I wish I could say that I am good at praying that way, but the truth is, I tend to be more like Martha.

As stated before, I know there are people who could be serving and are not, and the reason is simply laziness or lack of desire. Even if that is the case, it still isn't right for me to lash out in anger and frustration. It isn't proper for me to demand that God make them serve. Rather, it is my job as a sister in Christ to encourage their hearts and pray that God would soften them to hear His voice and cause them to want to serve Jesus.

These are the times that I must remember that I am only accountable for me, and while I can pray for people and spur them on, I can't make them serve. When I react out of frustration, my heart may want what is right, but my attitude is in the wrong place.

Such was the case with Martha—she had a heart for service, and she was frustrated that her sister seemingly did not. She wanted to make sure that Jesus was served properly as a guest in her home. What she failed to see was that, "There are different kinds of service, but the same Lord" (1 Corinthians 12:5). Mary was indeed serving the Lord, just not in the same way that Martha was. Mary's service was worship and adoration, learning from the Savior how to sit quietly and hear His wisdom. Martha could not see past the importance of her own service to see that what Mary was doing was just as important. In fact, Jesus said, "Mary has chosen what is better, and it will not be taken from her" (Luke 10:42).

Eliminate Pride

The bottom line is that when we start to allow ourselves to fall into the unhealthy patterns of thinking that were described in the last two chapters, we will ultimately get frustrated, lose our focus on the Lord, and start lashing out. When we start to think that God doesn't see or care what we are doing or we feel like we are doing the work alone, it causes us to reach a breaking point of saying to God, "Make them do something!"

What is really happening in that moment is that we have taken our focus off of God and put it onto ourselves. We have made our service all about us and what we are doing instead of what God is doing through us. That is the very definition of pride.

Galatians 6:3-4 says,

If anyone thinks they are something when they are not, they deceive themselves. Each one should test their own actions. Then they can take pride in themselves alone, without comparing themselves to someone else.

There are four takeaways that I see in this passage of Scripture: 1) don't puff yourself up; 2) worry only about yourself; 3) take pride in your work, but not worldly, human pride; and 4) don't compare yourself to others.

Let's take a deeper look at the parable that was mentioned in the last chapter about the Pharisee and the tax collector. The Pharisee's behavior is a prime example of what happens when we don't follow these four principles. When you read carefully, you can see that he was falling short in these areas mentioned in Galatians 6:3-4.

The Pharisee puffed himself up by reciting a list before God of all of the acts of service he was performing. He made sure to point out others who were not serving as well as he was instead of being concerned about himself and his walk with the Lord. He took human pride in his work, pride that focused everything on himself instead of how God was working through him.

Finally, he compared himself to the tax collector to make himself feel more worthy before God. This Pharisee's prayer was all about himself without a single thought that maybe the attitude of his heart needed adjusting. It was all about the service he was performing and the lack of service of others, especially the tax collector.

When we start to get frustrated with those around us not pulling their weight or not serving God the way we think they should, we become like the Pharisee. We tell God all the ways we are serving and demand that He make others work too. We forget that the work we do is actually God working through us, and that we can do nothing without Christ (John 15:5). We begin to exalt ourselves instead of showing the humility that God requires. This is when we need an attitude adjustment of the heart.

Take on Jesus' Attitude

The best way to get this attitude adjustment is to take on the mindset of Jesus Himself. Read the following passage from Philippians 2:3-8:

Do nothing out of selfish ambition or vain conceit. Rather, in humility value others above yourselves, not looking to your own interests but each of you to the interests of the others. In your relationships with others, have the same mindset as Christ Jesus:

Who, being in very nature God, did not consider equality with God something to be used to his own advantage; rather, he made himself nothing by taking the very nature of a servant, being made in human likeness. And being found in appearance as a man, he humbled himself by becoming obedient to death—even death on a cross!

How do we look beyond others' faults and stop worrying about who is working the hardest in the body of Christ? We value others above ourselves and look to the interest of others instead of our own.

Look back over that passage and notice some key aspects of Jesus' attitude. First, He was God in the flesh, but He did not consider Himself equal with God. He had every right to, but when He became human, He chose to give that up for you and me. Also, He made Himself nothing and took on the role of a servant.

Think about that—the God of the universe, Creator of everything, became a servant to the ones who should have been serving Him. Then He humbled Himself enough to be nailed to a cross and die so that you and I could have eternal life with the Father. He gave up His throne in glory, His place beside the Father, so that we could have our place for eternity.

Be a Servant

The perfect example of this humble service is found in John 13:1-17. Jesus, knowing that He was about to go to the cross and suffer for the sins of the world, decided to take on the role of a servant and wash the disciples' feet. This may seem like an odd act of service to us today, but in that culture, this job was reserved for the servants of the house, and it wasn't a pleasant one.

As people walked along the roads, they picked up dirt on their feet. They might also step in animal droppings or rotten food. So when individuals entered a person's house, a servant would wash their feet. Guests would never wash their own feet, and the master of the house certainly wouldn't do this disgusting job.

Yet here we see Jesus, Master of the whole universe, voluntarily and willingly taking on the task of washing feet. Then, in verses 12-17, He explained why He did this. It was to set an example for us of how we are to treat each other. He wanted His disciples—and us—to see that if we are going to truly represent Him, we must humble ourselves and be willing to serve one another, even when that service is messy and unpleasant, and even when others are not doing their part.

Take some time to allow all of that to sink in. Look at the example that Jesus left for us, and realize that He told us to have that same attitude of humility. So often when we serve the Lord, we notice that others are not serving, and instead of putting on humility we put on frustration.

In a perfect world, everyone would use their gifts and talents for the Lord and would serve Him and others exactly the way God intended. We don't live in a perfect world, at least not yet. So, of course, there are going to be those who have gifts and talents they are not using while others have the ability to serve in a certain area and just don't want to.

Teach and Admonish in Love

It isn't sinful or ungodly to teach people to use their gifts and talents and that idleness is not what God intends for us. We need to be guiding people into His service. However, saying "Tell them to serve you!" is not the way to go about helping people learn this principle. When we want people to serve simply because we are frustrated that we are doing more than they are, we are not trying to reach them out of a heart for Christ, but out of our own pride. Instead, we should practice Colossians 3:12-17:

> *Therefore, as God's chosen people, holy and dearly loved, clothe yourselves with compassion, kindness, humility, gentleness and patience. Bear with each other and forgive one another if any of you has a grievance against someone. Forgive as the Lord forgave you. And over all these virtues put on love, which binds them all together in perfect unity.*

> *Let the peace of Christ rule in your hearts, since as members of one body you were called to peace. And be thankful. Let the message of Christ dwell among you richly as you teach and admonish one another with all wisdom through psalms, hymns, and songs from the Spirit, singing to God with gratitude in your hearts. And whatever you do, whether in word or deed, do it all in the name of the Lord Jesus, giving thanks to God the Father through him.*

In this passage, we are clearly told to teach and admonish each other, but take a close look at how we are to do those things. We first need to be clothed, or covered, in all of the virtues that Jesus has: compassion, kindness, humility, gentleness, and patience. Until we take off our own pride and put on those virtues, we will not be able to live out the rest of this passage.

Once we make this exchange, the next step is to forgive others, and then, most important of all, to love them. After we have done all of this, then we can teach and admonish others, but only in that love that we've put on.

Truthfully, we cannot be effective teachers to others about

Christ's message until we have taken care of our own hearts first. Remember what Jesus said in Matthew 7:5: "First, take the plank out of your own eye, and then you will see clearly to remove the speck from your brother's eye." How much better we would be if we just stopped looking for that speck in others' eyes to begin with and focused on our own hearts!

Don't get me wrong, we need to help others to see the error of their ways. The verse above indicates that we do need to "Remove the speck from your brother's eye." We need to spur each other on to work for the Lord, but we can't see clearly to do that if we have not examined ourselves first. There is no way to help others if our attitude is one of pride or frustration.

Mary, Martha, and Us

Before moving on to the next chapters of this book, take one last look at what Martha said to Jesus. Remember through all of this Martha meant well—her desire was to serve the Lord, and she went to Jesus with that desire. Everything she said in this statement, from "Don't you care, Lord" to "She isn't working for you" to "Tell her to help me" came from a heart of wanting to see her sister serve as well.

What she needed was for Jesus to gently teach her what was better, and He was about to do just that. Watch the interaction that unfolds between these women and their Savior, and be amazed at how wonderfully Jesus teaches us what is better.

Balance Your Mary and Martha

Sit at His Feet

I'm sure we all have those people in our Christian family who have frustrated us because they seem to be spiritually lazy. Sit quietly with the Lord and His Word, and ask Him to show you the best way to deal with this frustration and how to gently guide those people into service for Him. Ask Him to forgive you for any negative feelings you've had toward your fellow believers.

Meditate on the following verses as you sit at His feet:

- 1 Corinthians 12:5 – "There are different kinds of service, but the same Lord."
- Colossians 3:15 – "Let the peace of Christ rule in your hearts, since as members of one body you were called to peace."
- Philippians 2:4 – "Not looking to your own interests but each of you to the interests of the others."

Learn from Him

Take some time to think about and journal what you read in this chapter. Use the following questions to guide your thoughts.

- Have you been frustrated with someone's lack of service? How can you move from an attitude of "Make them serve you" to an attitude of encouragement and a gentle spurring?
- Look again at the four principles taught in Galatians 6. Do you struggle with any of those? What steps can you take to give that over to the Lord and practice humility?
- Why is it so important to adjust our own hearts and attitudes before we try to spur others on to good works?

Serve Him

Take the time to put on the qualities listed in Colossians 3:12-17. Take off any hard feelings you've been holding against someone and put on love. When God shows you it is appropriate, approach that person who you think is not serving the Lord. Have a gentle, loving conversation and guide them into finding their spiritual gifts. Help plug them in to a ministry.

Put these passages of Scripture into practice as you serve Him:

- Colossians 3:12 – "Let the message of Christ dwell among you richly as you teach and admonish one another."

- Colossians 3:17 – "And whatever you do, whether in word or deed, do it all in the name of the Lord Jesus, giving thanks to God the Father through him."

- Galatians 6:2 – "Carry each other's burdens, and in this way you will fulfill the law of Christ."

8

He Calls Us by Name

"Martha, Martha," the Lord answered (Luke 10:41a).

What a beautiful way that Jesus addressed Martha! After sitting quietly and listening to her outcry of feeling frustrated that she was working by herself while her sister sat, He calmly and lovingly called her by name. We serve such a loving Savior! In Psalm 147:4 we are told, "He determines the numbers of the stars and calls them each by name."

Just think of the billions and billions of stars in this universe; He doesn't just know the names of those, He knows *your* name, too. He says in Isaiah 43:1, "But now, this is what the Lord says—he who created you, Jacob, he who formed you, Israel: 'Do not fear, for I have redeemed you; I have summoned you by name; you are mine.'"

Try reading that verse in a personal way, putting your name in where it says "Jacob" and "Israel." Understand that just as God redeemed and summoned Israel, He redeems and summons you. He calls you by name, and if you have accepted Christ as your Savior, He says, "You are mine." Out of the billions of people on this planet, He knows you individually. He knows your name.

Remembering Names

Knowing my own limitations, this fact about Jesus amazes me. If you are like me, remembering names is a challenge. I have to meet and interact with someone at least twice before I will remember the person's name. Even when I make a conscious effort and try to connect the name with something so I'll remember it, it feels like they're not out of my presence for five minutes and their name is already gone.

I've gotten into the habit when I meet new people to apologize in advance and tell them that the next time we meet I will most likely have to ask them their name again. Although I've been teaching for over twenty years, I even struggle learning my new students' names. I have to spend the first couple weeks of school adhering to a strict seating chart so that I can put faces with names. I wish I were better at it, but it is just not my strong suit.

I realize, however, that remembering a person's name is important. I know from experience how much nicer it feels when someone remembers my name. It makes me feel like I am important to them when they've taken the effort to learn my name and use it to address me. It shows that they want to know me as an individual, not just another acquaintance on a list.

I know that my students feel like I value them when I take the time to learn their names and use them to call on them in class. It isn't that I don't try to learn people's names, and it isn't that I don't realize the importance of it. I'm just not good at it.

Thankfully, Jesus isn't like me. He knew your name long before you were even born, and He will never forget it. Let's explore some Scriptures that tell us just how well our Savior knows us and how He calls us by name. I pray as you read these passages that you will understand just how deeply you are loved by Jesus and how much He desires to have a personal, intimate relationship with you.

You Are Fully Known

First, consider Jeremiah 1:5: "Before I formed you in the womb I knew you, before you were born I set you apart; I appointed you as a prophet to the nations." Yes, this passage was written specifically for Jeremiah. But do you realize the Lord says the same about you? Before you were formed in the womb, He knew you. He formed you for a specific purpose.

For Jeremiah, that purpose was to be a prophet to the nations. For you, it is something specific that He will reveal to your heart if you'll let Him. For now, just realize that your Savior knew you even before you were a thought in your parents' minds—even before you were in the womb. You were set apart to have a purpose in His great plan before any human knew you would even exist.

Psalm 139:16 is another passage that shows that He knew us before we were born: "Your eyes saw my unformed body. All the days ordained for me were written in your book before one of them came to be." God knew all of your days before you were even born. He saw you in your mother's womb while you were still a single cell, an unformed body. And He knew even then when you would be born and when you would die. He knew all your days in between. He even knew in what ways you would stray from Him and when and how you would come back to Him. He knew it all, including your name.

If you think those passages are amazing, read this verse and contemplate the awesomeness of our God: "Even as he chose us in him before the foundation of the world, that we should be holy and blameless before him" (Ephesians 1:4). Did you catch that? He chose us *before the foundation of the world!* He knew your name before He ever created this earth you live in.

That is how well God knows you and how much He loves you. Before He ever created anything you see around you, He knew He would create you. The plan from beginning to end was already on His mind even before He created light, and He knew that you would be a part of that. When I stop and really think about that, I am blown away. He loves me so much that He had me placed into His grand design before the beginning of time. What an amazing love!

Called by Name

In this love, God calls us by name. Look at how He spoke to Martha in the focus verse for this chapter. He spoke her name twice, saying, "Martha, Martha, you are worried about many things..." (Luke 10:41). While this was an admonishment, it was not spoken out of anger, frustration, or impatience. This was Jesus lovingly speaking to Martha's heart to show her what was better. He loved Martha deeply and wanted her to feel that love by calling her by name. And by calling her name twice, He was sure to get her attention to let her know that He was about to tell her something especially important.

Let's look at another instance where Jesus called someone by name in order to express His love and get her attention. In John 20:1-18, on the third day after Jesus was crucified, Mary Magdalene went to the tomb to grieve his death. When she got there, she found that the stone had been rolled away and the body of Jesus was missing.

After the disciples came and saw and went back to where they were staying, Mary stayed at the entrance to the tomb crying. She thought that someone had come and taken Jesus' body. She simply couldn't bear the thought that not only had she lost her Lord in death, now she couldn't even pay her final respects.

This is where the story gets interesting. Mary looked into the tomb again, and there she saw two angels who asked her why she was crying. She didn't even flinch, but just answered their question saying, "They have taken my Lord away, and I don't know where they have put him" (John 20:13). Then she turned around, and there was Jesus standing before her, but she didn't know it was Him. He too asked her why she was crying. Wait a minute—Mary saw two angels, and then the risen Savior, and she didn't have any kind of reaction? How is that possible?

I think that Mary was so overwhelmed by grief that she could not comprehend what was happening. Scripture doesn't say what Mary thought about the angels in the tomb where Jesus had been laid, but it does tell us that she thought Jesus was the gardener.

This makes sense; after all, nobody was expecting to find Jesus alive. Mary was one of the people who had personally been present at the cross and watched Him die. This was a grief deeper than any she had ever known, and there was no way at first for her to understand all she was witnessing.

Look carefully at how Jesus addressed Mary in the garden. First, in John 20:15, he addressed her as "Woman." It was the same term the angels inside the tomb had used. I was taken aback by that at first; in our culture today, it can seem offensive for a woman to be addressed that way. However, in Jesus' day, it was a term of endearment.

The one difficulty we have in reading conversations that Jesus had with people is that we can't see facial expressions or body language, and we can't hear the tone of voice that He used. This was a very tender conversation. Jesus was about to reveal Himself to Mary as her risen Savior, and so He spoke to her with love and compassion.

In all her grief, Mary didn't recognize Jesus. Remember, she thought He was the gardener. This moment in John 20:16 became the most tender and loving part of this encounter. Imagine Jesus, with all of the gentleness and affection He had to offer, saying, "Mary."

Imagine Mary, turning toward Him with full recognition and falling at His feet in worship. Jesus called her by name, and in doing that, Mary knew that she mattered, that Jesus was alive, and all hope was not lost. All it took was one word—her name.

You Are Intimately Known

The kind and understanding way in which Jesus spoke to Martha when she was upset by her sister not helping and the way Jesus spoke to Mary in the garden, is the same way He speaks to us. With all tenderness and compassion, our Savior calls us by name.

He wants to know us, and us to know Him, in a personal and intimate way. Each individual believer is special to Him. In John 10, Jesus refers to Himself as the Good Shepherd and to us as His sheep. In verse 3, He says that "He calls His own sheep by name and leads them out."

It is easy for us to think of ourselves as just one person in a sea of billions of people on this earth, one sheep in the middle of a huge flock. It is easy to feel like we don't have much significance in the grand scheme of things. But just picture the analogy that Jesus makes in John 10. Jesus is the Shepherd of all His sheep.

He doesn't just open the gate and herd them out as one big mass and then leave them on their own to figure it out. No, He calls each one by name and leads them out. He speaks individually, personally, to each one so they know where to go.

Read and ponder the words of Psalm 23:

The Lord is my shepherd, I lack nothing. he makes me lie down in green pastures, he leads me beside quiet waters, he refreshes my soul. He guides me along the right paths for his name's sake. Even though I walk through the darkest valley, I will fear no evil, for you are with me; your rod and your staff, they comfort me. You prepare a table before me in the presence of my enemies. You anoint my head with oil; my cup overflows. Surely your goodness and love will follow me all the days of my life, and I will dwell in the house of the Lord forever.

This psalm is all about the Good Shepherd, leading His sheep and caring for them. Notice the psalm is not about the herd being led, but the individual. All of the phrases depict one sheep being cared for by the Shepherd. Jesus does this for each one of His sheep. Yes, we are part of a larger flock, but our Savior knows every one of His special sheep by name, and He tenderly leads and guides each one individually.

This psalm is one of the most memorized passages of the Bible, and rightly so. However, sometimes a popular passage of Scripture such as this one becomes something we just recite, and we lose the meaning of it. Sit quietly with this psalm for a while, and let your Savior show you just how much you matter to Him and just how well He knows you. Allow this passage to become about you and your relationship to your Shepherd. Let Him call you by name and spend some intimate time with Him.

Mary, Martha, and Us

Go back now to what was happening between Jesus and Martha. Jesus was about to teach Martha some important truths about her relationship to Him. He was about to reach the moment where He showed her what was better. Instead of impatiently admonishing her, He slowed her busy mind by calling her by name, twice.

He lovingly invited her to listen to Him and understand that she was missing what was most important—quiet time with her Savior. The teaching that He provided for her next is one of the most important lessons for us to learn as well. But before He can teach us, He has to get us to slow down and listen to Him.

Just as He called to Martha to get her attention, He is calling us. He is sitting at the table, waiting for us to join Him so that He can show us what is better. Come and sit at His feet and allow Him to teach you. Let Him show you the perfect love He has for you and give you strength for the service you will perform.

Balance Your Mary and Martha

Sit at His Feet

Take some time to read and meditate on the scriptures given in this chapter. Close your eyes and picture Jesus reaching out to you and calling you by name. Think about the depth of His love—that He knew you and chose you before the creation of the world. Give Him praise and adoration for His endless love for you.

Meditate on the following verses as you sit at His feet:

- Isaiah 43:1 – "Do not fear, for I have redeemed you; I have summoned you by name; you are mine."
- John 10:3 – "The sheep listen to his voice. He calls his own sheep by name and leads them out."
- Isaiah 49:1 – "From my mother's womb he has spoken my name."

Learn from Him

Take some time to think about and journal what you read in this chapter. Use the following questions to guide your thoughts.

- What thoughts or feelings do you have about all the passages of Scripture that speak of how well God knows you?
- What is the significance of Jesus using both Martha's and Mary Magdalene's name in His encounters with them?
- What new ideas or realizations came to mind as you sat quietly with Psalm 23?

Serve Him

Once you have a firm grasp on just how well Jesus knows you, go and share that information with others. Find friends or relatives that you know are struggling with this concept. Invite them to lunch or give them a phone call. Let them know what you have learned and show them that they can have the same thing. Help others find the perfect love of Christ, just as you have.

Put these passages of Scripture into practice as you serve Him:

- Acts 1:8 – "But you will receive power when the Holy Spirit comes on you; and you will be my witnesses."
- Psalm 23:1 – "The Lord is my shepherd, I lack nothing."
- Psalm 139:1 – "You have searched me, Lord, and you know me."

9

Do Not Worry

You are worried and upset about many things (Luke 10:41b).

Once Jesus called Martha by name and got her attention, He didn't waste any time getting to the root of the problem. Martha couldn't get her focus in the right place because she was worried and upset about *many* things. Jesus didn't ask her what was wrong or beat around the bush. He simply stated what He saw in her heart and actions—she was worried, and that worry was causing her to be upset and behave in ways she wouldn't normally behave.

We so often get into this same pattern of worrying, becoming upset, and then taking those emotions out on others. Remember in the previous chapters, we learned that unhealthy ways of thinking lead to unhealthy behaviors, such as lashing out at others or at God. Like Martha, we spiral into that pattern of thinking that God doesn't care, or that we are the only ones doing the work. And when we allow those thought patterns to roll over into our emotions, we start to take it out on others, or even on God Himself.

Jesus' Teaching

Jesus looks at all of these emotions and behaviors, and He says, "You are worried and upset about many things." But this is also exactly what He taught us not to do. During His famous Sermon on the Mount, Jesus spoke these words:

> *Therefore I tell you, do not worry about your life, what you will eat or drink; or about your body, what you will wear. Is not life more than food, and the body more than clothes? Look at the birds of the air; they do not sow or reap or store away in barns, and yet your heavenly Father feeds them. Are you not much more valuable than they? Can any one of you by worrying add a single hour to your life? And why do you worry about clothes? See how the flowers of the field grow. They do not labor or spin. Yet I tell you that not even Solomon in all his splendor was dressed like one of these. If that is how God clothes the grass of the field, which is here today and tomorrow is thrown into the fire, will he not much more clothe you—you of little faith? So do not worry, saying, "What shall we eat?" or "What shall we drink?" or "What shall we wear?" For the pagans run after all these things, and your heavenly Father knows that you need them. But seek first his kingdom and his righteousness, and all these things will be given to you as well. Therefore do not worry about tomorrow, for tomorrow will worry about itself. Each day has enough trouble of its own* (Matthew 6:25-34).

This segment of His sermon was specifically relating to His provision for us and how we do not have to worry about having what we need. There are a couple of key phrases, however, that go way deeper than that.

Consider this question: "Can any one of you by worrying add a single hour to your life?" Jesus knows that worry has all kinds of health implications. Worry impacts all areas of our health: physical, social, emotional, and spiritual. It can cause high blood pressure, anxiety, unwanted weight loss, or even weight gain due to "stress eating."

Worry can also cause us to get overly emotional and be in a bad mood and treat others poorly, harming our social health. Also, when we worry, we are not putting our trust in God, so it damages our spiritual health. So not only does worry not add hours to our lives, it actually subtracts them.

Take some time to ponder what Jesus was saying in the last two sentences in this part of His sermon. "Therefore do not worry about tomorrow, for tomorrow will worry about itself. Each day has enough trouble of its own." This has actually become my life verse. I have committed, although I am not perfect at it, to getting up every day and saying, "Whatever you have for me today, Lord, let's do it." I have come to the understanding that worrying about tomorrow strips today of the joy it should have.

Learning to Live Worry-Free

During the COVID years I really learned to live out this principle. At work I was in a position in which I had to sort out close contacts of those with positive cases, who had to quarantine, and how long that quarantine had to last. It felt like the phone rang nonstop, and each call was either someone who had tested positive or who was a close contact of a positive case.

I learned very quickly not to worry about who might call tomorrow, but to take each day, and even each call, as it came. I learned to just deal with the situation at hand and not worry about what else might come later on.

Consider the truth of that last phrase, "Each day has enough trouble of its own." Every day, we have circumstances we will need to face. Not every circumstance is bad; most of them are just part of everyday life. We have decisions to make, a schedule to keep, people to take care of, a job to do, meals to prepare, and so on. We have enough every single day to keep our minds occupied. We don't need to clutter our minds worrying about the future.

The Worry-Free Recipe

So what are we to do? Worrying is a natural human response when we're not sure about the outcomes of our circumstances. How do we break this bad habit of being "worried and upset" as Jesus described it to Martha? First, look back to the sermon in Matthew 6. After Jesus listed some things that we tend to worry about, He said, "But seek first his kingdom and his righteousness, and all these things will be given to you as well."

What Jesus is telling us is that the reason we worry is that we have our minds in the wrong place; we are seeking the wrong things. He promises that if we will just seek Him, He will give us everything else.

When all we can focus on is this life, these earthly needs and wants, we cannot put our focus on what really matters: Jesus. This was the problem with Martha. The problem wasn't her service. It was her focus. She was so distracted, worried, and upset that she had allowed her focus to be on all of the circumstances that were causing her emotions instead of focusing on Christ.

Notice, though, this one important word in what Jesus taught: first. He said to "Seek first his kingdom and his righteousness." It isn't wrong for us to know what our needs are and pursue them. It is a good thing to seek ways we can serve God and others. It is when we start to seek these things first instead of Jesus that it becomes a problem. This is when all of the attitudes and behaviors we talked about previously crop up, and it starts to become about *us* instead of *Him*.

Seek Him When You're Stressed

Let's take a look at how Jesus Himself handled anxiety and stress. In Mark 14:34, just before He was arrested, knowing all that was about to happen, we read, "'My soul is overwhelmed with sorrow to the point of death,' he said to them. 'Stay here and keep watch.'" This was a struggle that the human side of Jesus was not going to be able to handle. He was overwhelmed, shaken to the core with the knowledge of what He was going to have to suffer.

So what did He do with that worry? He took it directly to the feet of the Father. Notice what we are told in verses 35 and 36 of this same chapter: "Going a little farther, he fell to the ground and prayed that if possible the hour might pass from him. 'Abba, Father,' he said, 'everything is possible for you. Take this cup from me. Yet not what I will, but what you will.'"

Everything Jesus did while on this earth was an example for us to follow. Even while He was in the midst of anguish over what He was about to suffer, He showed us how to deal with that anguish. He did not allow His emotions to take over, but took His worry directly to the Father. He did not act according to human feelings or try to change things so that they would turn out better for Him, but rather went to God and laid it at His feet. None of it was about His own will; it was all about God's will.

Seek Him When You're Successful

Seeking the Lord first is not only important in the case of worry and anxiety. We also must seek Him first in our accomplishments. Colossians 3:2 tells us, "Set your mind on things above, not on earthly things." If we are not careful and intentional about seeking God first, if we set our minds on things of this earth, it will lead us down a path of relying on ourselves and turning from God. It is quite easy to fall into the trap of looking at our accomplishments and taking the credit for them instead of recognizing that it is God who provides all things, and we would have accomplished nothing without Him.

Think about the church at Laodicea in Revelation 3:14-22:

To the angel of the church in Laodicea write:

These are the words of the Amen, the faithful and true witness, the ruler of God's creation. I know your deeds, that you are neither cold nor hot. I wish you were either one or the other! So, because you are lukewarm—neither hot nor cold—I am about to spit you out of my mouth. You say, "I am rich; I have acquired wealth and do not need a thing." But you do not realize that you are wretched, pitiful, poor, blind and naked. I counsel you to buy from me gold refined in the fire, so you can become rich; and white clothes to wear, so you can cover your shameful nakedness; and salve to put on your eyes, so you can see. Those whom I love I rebuke and discipline. So be earnest and repent. Here I am! I stand at the door and knock. If anyone hears my voice and opens the door, I will come in and eat with that person, and they with me. To the one who is victorious, I will give the right to sit with me on my throne, just as I was victorious and sat down with my Father on his throne. Whoever has ears, let them hear what the Spirit says to the churches.

In verse 17, Jesus pointed out to these people how much they were relying on self instead of Him. He told them that they thought it was by their own power that they had acquired their wealth. He was quick to show them what He thought about this idea when He said, "But you do not realize that you are wretched, pitiful, poor, blind and naked."

Remember, this was Jesus speaking to a church—to Christians. This part of the body of Christ had become so focused on worldly things that they had forgotten who provided those things. They had taken all the credit for the wealth they had amassed, so Jesus told them, "You aren't rich at all. As a matter of fact, you are poor and wretched."

Now look at the consequences that Jesus described to this church because of their worldly attitude. He said to them in verse 16, "I am about to spit you out of my mouth." Thinking about how we normally fall into any sin, I don't think that the people of Laodicea got to this point overnight. I believe that it was little by little, losing focus here and there, until the total focus was off of God and onto themselves. They had forgotten, over time, to set their minds on things above.

The wonderful news of Christ comes at the end of this passage in verses 18-21: we don't have to stay in that place of putting ourselves first. Jesus will counsel us to return to Him, He will rebuke and discipline us in love to bring us to repentance. He will knock at the door of our hearts, and when we answer, He will come in and restore us. And those who are victorious over these attitudes will have the right to sit on His throne with Him.

Mary, Martha, and Us

Jesus had this same message to speak to Martha's heart, and to our hearts as well. Stop being worried and upset about so many things. Stop focusing on this world. Get your focus on the things that are unseen—all of the glory that awaits you in heaven. Realize that this world is not your home, that none of the worldly stuff is permanent.

This truth is where you find true peace and freedom from worry. Philippians 4:6-7 says,

Do not be anxious about anything, but in every situation, by prayer and petition, with thanksgiving, present your requests to God. And the peace of God, which transcends all understanding, will guard your hearts and minds in Christ Jesus.

Notice in the above passage that this peace only comes

through giving over your anxious heart to the Lord. He wants you to take every situation to Him—the big and the small—and let Him take the worry away. He wanted to do this for Martha, and He wants to do it for you as well.

In the next part of this account of Mary and Martha, Jesus would show Martha what is better. All of her anxiety, worry, and other emotions that were stirred up by her frustrations would melt away if she would just learn this lesson. The biggest lesson for Martha, and for us, was about to be revealed. Don't allow your worry to take over your relationship with Christ. Take Jesus' advice to seek His kingdom first, and let Him show you the only thing you need.

Come sit at the feet of Jesus with Mary and allow Him to speak to your heart. Like Mary, put the worries of this life aside and listen to what He has to say.

Balance Your Mary and Martha

Sit at His Feet

Take some time to read and meditate on Matthew 6:25-34. Spend some quiet time allowing Jesus to show you areas where you tend to worry. Let Him show you where you have been focusing more on this world than on Him. Confess those areas, repent, and let your heart be open to letting go of your worry and placing it at His feet.

Meditate on the following verses as you sit at His feet:

- Colossians 3:1-2 – "Since, then, you have been raised with Christ, set your hearts on things above, where Christ is, seated at the right hand of God."

- Matthew 6:33-34 – "Therefore do not worry about tomorrow…"

- Philippians 4:6-7 – "Do not be anxious about anything…"

Learn from Him

Take some time to think about and journal what you read in this chapter. Use the following questions to guide your thoughts.

- As you ponder the passage from Matthew above, what is God speaking to your heart? What is He asking you to give over to Him?

- Notice in the letter to the church in Laodicea, Jesus says He is about to spit them out of His mouth. How can we avoid hearing these same words from Jesus?

- How can you gain true peace that only comes from the Lord?

Serve Him

Once you have laid that burden of worry down, look for areas of ministry that you have been neglecting because you were allowing the worries of this life to stifle your service to the Lord. Is there a place you could be serving Him but you were too worried about your abilities or what others will think? Step out in faith and start serving in those areas He shows you.

Put these passages of Scripture into practice as you serve Him:

- Matthew 25:28 – "For whoever has will be given more, and they will have an abundance."

- Revelation 3:18 – "I counsel you to buy from me gold refined in the fire, so you can become rich; and white clothes to wear, so you can cover your shameful nakedness; and salve to put on your eyes, so you can see."

- Matthew 6:27 – "Can any one of you by worrying add a single hour to your life?

10

Jesus Is All You Need

But few things are needed—or indeed only one (Luke 10:42a).

In this part of Jesus' interaction with Mary and Martha, the main purpose for His visit became apparent. Here He taught the most important lesson in the entire account: Jesus is all you need. Let's put the whole statement together. "You are worried and upset about many things, but few things are needed—or indeed only one." Jesus was telling Martha, and He is telling us as well, that we are getting caught up in this world and what we think we need. However, there is nothing in this world that truly satisfies. Jesus is all we need.

Remember what Jesus said in Matthew 6: "But seek first his kingdom and his righteousness, and all these things will be given to you as well" (Matthew 6:33). We've already discussed the importance of seeking Him first. Now look at the results of putting that into practice.

All of those things that you have been worrying about and striving for will be given to you when you seek Him first. Some of what you are striving for—the worldly pleasures you really don't need—will melt away as you realize where true pleasure comes from. If you have Jesus, you have everything you need.

All-In Faith

Jesus had some straightforward and difficult teaching on this subject. In Luke 14:25-33, we read the following:

Large crowds were traveling with Jesus, and turning to them he said: "If anyone comes to me and does not hate father and mother, wife and children, brothers and sisters— yes, even their own life—such a person cannot be my disciple. And whoever does not carry their cross and follow me cannot be my disciple. Suppose one of you wants to build a tower. Won't you first sit down and estimate the cost to see if you have enough money to complete it? For if you lay the foundation and are not able to finish it, everyone who sees it will ridicule you, saying, 'This person began to build and wasn't able to finish.' "Or suppose a king is about to go to war against another king. Won't he first sit down and consider whether he is able with ten thousand men to oppose the one coming against him with twenty thousand? If he is not able, he will send a delegation while the other is still a long way off and will ask for terms of peace. In the same way, those of you who do not give up everything you have cannot be my disciples. Salt is good, but if it loses its saltiness, how can it be made salty again? It is fit neither for the soil nor for the manure pile; it is thrown out. Whoever has ears to hear, let them hear."

We have so much to unpack in this teaching of Jesus. Let's look at it together, one step at a time. First, notice this: there were large crowds following Jesus. That seems great, doesn't it? Jesus was gaining a great following. But Jesus knew their hearts. He knew that many in that crowd were only there because they wanted to see the next miracle. For them, it was like a carnival sideshow—what cool thing might Jesus do next?

Others in the crowd just wanted to see what Jesus could do

for them personally. They wanted their diseases healed and their demons cast out, and once they got their personal miracle, they would move on with their lives. That is, until the next problem cropped up. Then they would seek Him again, get the healing they needed, and once again move on to live their lives.

This was never Jesus' intention for those who follow Him. He is looking for people who are all in, totally devoted. He wants disciples who realize that He is all they need for all areas of life. He wants followers who understand that all of their needs are fulfilled in Him. So when He saw these large crowds, He was totally up front and honest about what His expectations were.

I'm Supposed to Hate?

But those expectations were harsh—if you're going to follow me, He said, you must hate your family and your life. Wait a minute. Is this Savior, who preached love for your neighbor, asking you to hate your family if you are going to follow Him? That just doesn't make sense. This is one of those instances where you have to look at the whole character of Jesus, not just this one statement, to find the meaning behind what He was saying.

Remember that the character of Jesus never changes. He is loving, kind, compassionate, and full of grace. He would never ask you to hate anyone, especially your own family. The point He was trying to make to this crowd is that you must come to the realization that if you follow Him, He will fulfill your every need.

He wants you to see that no earthly thing, no matter how much we love it, can ever satisfy the needs of our soul. Only Jesus can do that. And so the love we have for these earthly things (yes even the love for our families), when compared to the love we have in Christ, looks like hate. It just can't ever measure up; really, it can't even be compared.

Jesus wanted to give this crowd, and us, a glimpse of eternity.

We tend to be so earthly focused that we have a tough time grasping how different eternity will be for us. You see, as much as we love and need family and friends on this earth, we will no longer need those things in heaven. It will be an amazing blessing that we still have our earthly relationships, but they won't be a need.

We are definitely created with a need for fellowship and companionship, but ultimately our need can only be fulfilled in Christ. We have the amazing gift of relationships with other people while we are here on earth, but those relationships can never compare with the perfect fellowship we will have with Jesus in eternity. People here on earth, even those we love dearly, still have the potential to disappoint us. Jesus will never do that; our relationship to Him is the only perfect one we will ever experience.

Jesus spoke of this difference between relationships in heaven and on earth in Matthew 22. In verses 23-28, The Sadducees had come to question Jesus about a hypothetical woman who was married. When her husband died, his brother married the woman. Then he died, and another brother married her. This went on through seven brothers. Keep in mind that it was the custom of the day for marriages to be arranged this way. The point that the Sadducees were trying to make with their story was that now this woman had eight different husbands, so whose wife would she be at the resurrection?

We find Jesus' answer to their question in verse 29-30: "Jesus replied, 'You are in error because you do not know the Scriptures or the power of God. At the resurrection people will neither marry nor be given in marriage; they will be like the angels in heaven.'"

In heaven, unlike on earth, we will have no need for human fellowship because we will be in perfect fellowship with our Savior. Our main purpose in heaven will be to honor and worship our God, and the needs that we have here on earth will disappear.

Don't let that discourage you. I know we look forward to the day when we will see our loved ones who have passed on before us. We will get that glorious reunion, and we will have that sweet fellowship. It just won't be a need. Every need will be fulfilled because we will have Jesus Himself. That is what Jesus wants us to understand when He says that we should "hate" our families. The love and reverence we have for Christ so outweighs our love for human companionship that it looks like hate in comparison. He is all we need!

Take Up Your Cross

Looking further in this passage from Luke 14, we see that Jesus also spoke about the fact that we must carry our cross and follow Him if we want to be His disciples. This is an all-in kind of faith, one that requires sacrifice. Jesus does not want us to suffer as we walk through this life with Him, but He knows that we will. He understands this world we live in; He knows it is fallen and sinful, and He knows that not everyone will want to follow Him. Those that do make that choice will face skepticism, ridicule, and downright hatred at times.

Taking up your cross also signifies death—dying to your own wants and desires and coming alive with desires that match what Jesus wants for you. This self-denial is much more than just saying "no" to yourself. It is a realization that you no longer own yourself. Paul explains in Romans 6:15-18 that you will be a slave to one of two things: sin or righteousness.

When you live for yourself and your own desires, you are a slave to sin; but when you take up your cross and follow Jesus, you become a slave to righteousness. This is not the type of bondage where you are forced to obey out of fear. Rather, it is a giving of your life over to the one who took your sin upon Himself. It is willing obedience, knowing that it is the better way.

A beautiful picture of this type of servitude can be found in Exodus 21:1-5. In this case, the law said that a Hebrew servant could be bought and would serve for six years, but in the seventh year, he was to be set free. But pay attention to verse 5. Sometimes the servant loved his master and wanted to stay with him and his family. He would choose to stay on as a servant, and he would be in that position for life.

In that case, he was serving out of willingness and love for his master. That is the type of slavery to righteousness Paul is talking about in Romans 6. It is not a life that is forced upon you. It is a life given over because of love for the Master, knowing what He has done for you. It is understanding that He is all you need.

Make an Informed Decision

The very next thing Jesus taught in this Luke 14 passage is the cost of becoming a disciple. Again, He was very up front and honest about what it would take to follow Him. Here He gives two examples: a person building a tower and a king going to war. In both instances, He says that nobody would do either of these things without first sitting down and figuring out what the cost would be. Anyone taking on such a task would want to make sure they could be successful before starting the venture.

The same holds true for following Jesus. He wants you to make an informed decision. He wants you to understand that following Him will not always be an easy road, and it will require sacrifice. In Luke 14:33, He says, "In the same way, those of you who do not give up everything you have cannot be my disciples." Does He mean that you can't have anything in this life? Of course not. What He does mean is that to be a true follower of Him, you must recognize that He is all you need.

You are giving everything up to Him and letting Him decide if it is necessary or not. You are acknowledging that He owns it all, and He has control of it, not you. You are admitting that "You are not your own; you were bought at a price" (1 Corinthians 6:19-20), and that price was Jesus' life, laid down for you.

Stay Salty

The final teaching in this passage seems, at first glance, to not fit in with the rest. What did Jesus mean when He spoke of salt losing its saltiness? First remember that in Matthew 5:13, as part of His sermon on the mount, Jesus said, "You are the salt of the earth." Consider two common uses for salt: to preserve and to add flavor. This is what Jesus expects of His followers. He wants us to preserve His teaching and spread the flavor of the Gospel all over the earth.

How does the salt lose its saltiness? It happens when believers start to take their focus off of Christ and start to worry about the things of this world. It happens when we forget that Jesus is all we need. Both Matthew 5 and Luke 14 indicate that this salt is no longer good for anything. We cannot be focused both on this world and on Christ and still be effective disciples.

We see this teaching in both Matthew 6:24 and Luke 16:13 where Jesus says,

No one can serve two masters. Either you will hate the one and love the other, or you will be devoted to the one and despise the other. You cannot serve both God and money.

It is impossible for us to be devoted to Christ and the world at the same time. Until we come to the realization that Jesus is all we need and start viewing the things of this world as His, not ours, we cannot be devoted disciples of Jesus.

Our Deepest Need

Don't forget our deepest need—salvation. We need to have our sins forgiven so that we can have eternal life. This need is only fulfilled in Christ. Apart from Him, there is no forgiveness, and we are still in our sin. But, praise God! Jesus died on the cross and rose from the dead so that we could have this deep need fulfilled. Hebrews 7:26, when talking about Jesus as our High Priest, says it this way, "Such a high priest truly meets our need—one who is holy, blameless, pure, set apart from sinners, exalted above the heavens."

Jesus will fulfill our physical needs, but it is not these worldly needs that are the most important. It is the eternal need of the soul, the need to have our sins forgiven, that is most important. This life and all of the physical things in it are temporary. Our problems, struggles, and worries, when compared with eternity, are short-lived.

God cares about these physical needs and trials, but He cares much more about the condition of your soul and where you spend eternity. Allow Jesus to fill this need in your life. Accept Him as your Savior and make Him Lord of your life. He is all you need.

Mary, Martha, and Us

Return with me to this chapter's focus verse and the conversation between Jesus and Martha. In Luke 10:41-42, He said, "You are worried and upset about many things, but few things are needed—or indeed only one." Jesus so desperately wanted Martha to understand that the only thing she needed was Him. Everything else would be provided if she just put her trust and faith in Jesus. There was no need to be worried and upset.

The next thing Jesus said to Martha was, "Mary has chosen what is better." Remember from previous chapters in this book that Martha's service was important, and that Jesus expects us to work for Him. But also remember that, unless the focus is on Him during those acts of service, the work will become worldly and burdensome. This was the lesson for Martha in her encounter with Jesus, and it is the lesson for us today. Jesus has to be at the center of everything. He must be all we need if we are going to serve Him properly.

Let us continue on in this encounter in the home of Mary and Martha so we can learn how to choose what is better.

Balance Your Mary and Martha

Sit at His Feet

Ask Jesus to reveal any areas in your life you have not surrendered to His control. Acknowledge that He owns it all, and give Him ownership of anything you've been holding onto. These could be physical objects, sins, attitudes, hobbies, ministries, your time, or anything else that you are not allowing Him to control. Let Him speak to your heart; then surrender to Him.

Meditate on the following verses as you sit at His feet:

- Luke 14:27 – "And whoever does not carry their cross and follow me cannot be my disciple."
- Proverbs 19:21 – "Many are the plans in a person's heart, but it is the Lord's purpose that prevails."
- Job 12:10 – "In his hand is…the breath of all mankind."

Learn from Him

Take some time to think about and journal what you read in this chapter. Use the following questions to guide your thoughts.

- When you think about the cost of following Jesus, what areas do you find most challenging?
- What steps do you need to take to become a "slave to righteousness"? What do you need to give up ownership of so that Jesus can take over and be all you need?
- In what areas have you lost your "saltiness"? What do you need to do to get it back?

Serve Him

Once you have settled with the Lord the things that you need to give over, look for ways to work for Him, being careful to be Spirit-led. Be sure that whatever you choose to do, it is for Him and by Him, not your own ideas or methods. Surrender your service to Him along with everything else.

Put these passages of Scripture into practice as you serve Him:

- Matthew 6:24 - "No one can serve two masters. Either you will hate the one and love the other, or you will be devoted to the one and despise the other. You cannot serve both God and money."

- Proverbs 16:9 – "In their hearts humans plan their course, but the Lord establishes their steps."

- John 15:8 – "This is to my Father's glory, that you bear much fruit, showing yourselves to be my disciples."

11

Choose Jesus First

Mary has chosen what is better, and it will not be taken away from her (Luke 10:42b).

In the church and in our lives, we think that the busyness of serving Jesus is what's important. The more we are doing for the Lord, the more rewards we get in heaven, right? While we will be given rewards for faithful service, and that service is important, it's our devotion to Christ that must be preeminent.

In this part of Jesus' interaction with Mary and Martha, Jesus made it plain to Martha that Mary had made the better choice. Two concepts become abundantly clear from this conversation: choosing Jesus is always better than any other choice, and once you have chosen Him, nobody can take Him from you.

Effective Service

As was mentioned in previous chapters, you cannot effectively serve until you have sat at the feet of Jesus and received what He has to say to you. Likewise, all of the service in the world is meaningless unless you have a devotion to Christ behind it. It doesn't matter what you do for the Lord if it isn't flowing out of a heart of faithfulness and love for your Savior.

Consider what Jesus taught in Matthew 7:21-23:

Not everyone who says to me, "Lord, Lord," will enter the kingdom of heaven, but only the one who does the will of my Father who is in heaven. Many will say to me on that day, "Lord, Lord, did we not prophesy in your name and in your name drive out demons and in your name perform many miracles?" Then I will tell them plainly, "I never knew you. Away from me, you evildoers!"

Here Jesus is giving an example of those who were most definitely working for Him. They were driving out demons and performing miracles, all in the name of Jesus. They even called Him Lord. So what was the problem? It was that these people were doing these works, keeping busy with all of the things they needed to "do" for Jesus, but they weren't devoted to Him. They weren't concerned about nurturing a personal relationship with Him but only doing the work.

There seems to be another problem here as well. These people were prophesying, driving out demons, and performing miracles, but preaching and teaching the Gospel was nowhere on that list. It seems as if these people were possibly doing all of these things so that they would be noticed, not so that Christ would be known. When our works become about us instead of Christ, we have neglected what is better.

Jesus went on in Matthew chapter 7, saying these words in verses 24-27:

Therefore everyone who hears these words of mine and puts them into practice is like a wise man who built his house on the rock. The rain came down, the streams rose, and the winds blew and beat against that house; yet it did not fall, because it had its foundation on the rock. But everyone who hears these words of mine and does not put them into practice is like a foolish man who built his house on sand. The rain came down, the streams rose, and the winds blew and beat against that house, and it fell with a great crash.

In this passage, Jesus talked about two things: hearing the

word and putting it into practice. It is obvious that you cannot put something into practice that you haven't heard. But you also can't hear something without listening. And you can't listen to Jesus without sitting at His feet. This is why Jesus said that Mary chose what was better. She couldn't possibly know how to serve Him without first learning from Him and knowing Him.

Recipe for Effective Service

So how do we, like Mary, find what is better yet still fulfill our service to the Lord? Let's look at Romans 12:1-2 to learn some practical steps for choosing Jesus before service:

Therefore, I urge you, brothers and sisters, in view of God's mercy, to offer your bodies as a living sacrifice, holy and pleasing to God—this is your true and proper worship. Do not conform to the pattern of this world, but be transformed by the renewing of your mind. Then you will be able to test and approve what God's will is—his good, pleasing and perfect will.

First, we offer our bodies as living sacrifices to God. After receiving the atonement made for us through the blood of Christ, this must be the next step in our walk with Him. The first and foremost step must be salvation, choosing Jesus as Savior and having our sins wiped clean. Then the very next step is surrender, choosing Jesus as Lord and allowing Him to reign in our lives.

To choose what is better, we must allow Jesus to be both Savior and Lord. This is what a living sacrifice looks like: complete surrender of our lives. That includes our physical bodies, thoughts, actions, words, decisions—everything. Sit at the feet of Jesus with the following verses and allow this idea of the Lordship of Christ to sink deep into your heart:

- Galatians 2:20: "I have been crucified with Christ and I no longer live, but Christ lives in me. The life I now live in the body, I live by faith in the Son of God, who loved me and gave himself for me."

- 1 Corinthians 6:19-20: "Do you not know that your bodies are temples of the Holy Spirit, who is in you, whom you have received from God? You are not your own; you were bought at a price. Therefore honor God with your bodies."

These two passages describe what true surrender looks like—you are giving over ownership of your life to the Lord and understanding that it is no longer your life to live. Every moment, every day is His. I understand that this idea is hard to swallow at first. It seems so restrictive to say that someone else has control over your life. Let me encourage you to understand that complete surrender to the Lord actually makes you completely free.

Practicing Surrender

I had to learn this in my own life by putting it into practice, and I can testify that it was not easy. For twenty years, I had the same job and the same routine; my life was organized just the way I liked it and I knew what to expect. Then a series of unusual things started to happen in my life. There were some changes at my job that made me feel out of place, like I didn't belong there anymore. Then the Lord, seemingly out of nowhere, placed on my heart the idea to write my first book, *Our Road to Emmaus*. Both of these things were entirely out of my comfort zone—I like to know what's coming, to establish a routine and stick to it.

God, however, was about to disrupt that routine. It became more and more apparent that the job the Lord had placed me in for all of those years was changing, and my role and place there was changing with it. I decided to pull back to part time until I could discern what God wanted me to do.

Working less gave me time to focus on the book He had placed on my heart, so I spent my afternoons doing the work of writing and trying to get published. I had no idea at the time what God was doing with my future. I often wondered if I had done the right thing, but I felt a peace in my spirit about it and I was determined to wait for Him.

When it became evident that my book was going to be published, I knew there were some significant changes coming for me. I made the conscious decision right then that I would live out what God had taught me during the pandemic. I would wake up every day and the first words out of my mouth would be, "Whatever you have for me today, Lord, let's do it." .

That was not an easy thing to do, but when I truly surrendered, I never experienced more freedom than when I began to really live it out. Mostly, I was free from worrying about what was to come. I learned to just live for each day God had given me and not worry about anything that the future held. Yes, I still prayed for the things I wanted to see happen, but I prayed that God would work them out in His way and His timing, not my own.

He did just that, in ways I would have never expected. My prayer was that things would work out at my job, that He would turn things around and place me back where I had always loved to work. I had been there for so long, and I really felt like it was where He had planted me. But sometimes God's plans are not our plans, and His plans are always better.

What God had intended, however, was for me to move on to another job in the same field, doing what I love to do and feeling free from the burden of the struggles I was having at the first job. I also prayed for my book to be published, for me to get the words out that I knew He had put on my heart. And in a whirlwind of exciting connections, He did just that.

None of this happened because of my own strength or my own work. I am convinced that these blessings poured out in my life because I chose to surrender. I chose to be the living sacrifice to God that is spoken of in Romans 12. I'm still not perfect at it, but I find that letting God be in control of each day has made me free in all kinds of ways.

Not only am I free from the worry about the future, but I have found myself being more open to things that I would have turned down before. I have found the freedom that Jesus spoke about in John 8:36 when He said, "So if the Son sets you free, you will be free indeed." Like Romans 12:1 says, I have found the "true and proper worship" of Jesus—the worship of giving over my life to Him and allowing everything I do to be grounded in Him and His Word.

Recipe for Surrender

So how do you get there? How do you surrender your life day after day to God's will and find that true and proper worship? I believe the recipe is found in Romans 12:2: "Do not conform to the pattern of this world, but be transformed by the renewing of your mind." Let's start with the first part—not conforming to the pattern of this world. This world has a pattern of worry and self-centeredness.

People go out of their way to get what they want when they want it. James called out believers when he said this in chapter 4 verses 2-3:

You desire but do not have, so you kill. You covet but you cannot get what you want, so you quarrel and fight. You do not have because you do not ask God. When you ask, you do not receive, because you ask with wrong motives, that you may spend what you get on your pleasures.

This is the pattern that Paul warns about in the Romans 12 passage. The world quarrels and fights, but why? Because there is something that they want, some self-centered need that is not fulfilled. And why can't they get that desire filled? Because they do not ask God. Even when they do ask, the motive behind the prayer is selfish, so they still do not receive.

Be careful, though, to not pin this behavior on only non-believers. If you look at the first two verses of James, you will see that he was writing to "the twelve tribes scattered among the nations" and to "brothers." James was writing to Christians who were living out of their self-centeredness. When we forget to follow the example of Mary and sit at the feet of Jesus and learn from Him, we are prone to start conforming to the pattern of this world. Like Mary, choose what is better, and practice the second part of Romans 12:2: "Be transformed by the renewing of your mind."

The only way to have your mind transformed and renewed is to daily choose what is better, sit quietly in the Word, and learn from your Savior. We live in the flesh, and we will think and act according to the flesh until our minds are transformed by the power of the Word. Do you want to live out the will of God and be obedient to Him? If so, then look closely again at Romans 12:2.

You have to have your mind transformed and renewed because it is then, and only then, that you will be able to "test and approve what God's will is." And the only way to have that transformation is to daily choose what is better. Each and every day, choose to sit at the feet of Jesus. Intentionally set aside time to learn from the Savior. Give over your whole life—everything that happens every day—to Him.

Mary, Martha, and Us

Keep in mind, though, that faith absolutely requires action. James 2:17 says, "In the same way, faith by itself, if it is not accompanied by action, is dead." Choosing what is better does not mean that we lay Martha aside and only follow the example of Mary. It means that we choose to cultivate our relationship with Jesus first and let the acts of service flow out of that relationship.

It also means surrendering our lives to Christ so that our service is not our idea, but rather what He wants us doing. When Christ is truly at the center, when He is Lord of our lives, sitting at His feet and serving Him will go hand in hand.

Take the time to fully grasp this before moving on to the next chapter. Put Jesus at the center of everything and fully surrender your life to Him. This is what Mary and Martha were learning, and what we need to learn as well. Choose what is better, and you will find that, just like Mary, it will not be taken from you.

Balance Your Mary and Martha

Sit at His Feet

Commit today to intentionally cultivating your relationship with Jesus. Set aside time to read the Bible and pray, and as you sit at His feet, ask Him to transform you through the renewing of your mind and make you think more like Him. Ask Jesus to give you His attitude, His thoughts, and His direction.

Meditate on the following verses as you sit at His feet:

- 1 Corinthians 2:16 – "…But we have the mind of Christ."

- Philippians 2:5 – "In your relationships with one another, have the same mindset as Christ Jesus."

- Galatians 2:20 – "I have been crucified with Christ and I no longer live, but Christ lives in me."

Learn from Him

Take some time to think about and journal what you read in this chapter. Use the following questions to guide your thoughts.

- In what ways have you jumped into service for the Lord without first sitting at His feet? How can you be sure to avoid this in the future?

- What steps do you need to take in order to live one day at a time with Jesus? How can you truly surrender your plans to Him and trust Him with your future?

- How do Galatians 2:20 and 1 Corinthians 6:19-20 encourage you to practice surrender to Jesus every day?

Serve Him

As Jesus begins to transform you, look for open doors of ministry where you can serve Him. Don't try to come up with ideas on your own, just watch for opportunities and grab them, performing them in His strength and wisdom. Remember that your service to Him will be so much better when it flows from your relationship with Him instead of it feeling like an obligation.

Put these passages of Scripture into practice as you serve Him:

- Matthew 7:24 – "Therefore everyone who hears these words of mine and puts them into practice is like a wise man who built his house on the rock."

- Philippians 1:6 – "He who began a good work in you will carry it on to completion until the day of Christ Jesus."

- Luke 6:43-45 – "A good man brings good things out of the good stored up in his heart, and an evil man brings evil things out of the evil stored up in his heart. For the mouth speaks what the heart is full of."

12

Nothing Can Separate

Mary has chosen what is better, and it will not be taken from her (Luke 10:42b).

Finding the balance between serving the Lord and sitting quietly at His feet is a journey indeed. It is a process of daily surrendering and getting closer and closer each day to saying, "Today—all of it—is Yours, Lord." And the beauty of knowing the Lord is that, once you choose this surrender, once you give your life to Jesus, it cannot be taken away from you.

Paul, in Romans 8:38-39, described it this way:

For I am convinced that neither death nor life, neither angels nor demons, neither the present nor the future, nor any powers, neither height nor depth, nor anything else in all creation, will be able to separate us from the love of God that is in Christ Jesus our Lord.

Nothing in this universe can take away the love of Christ once you have found it and grasped it for your own. This has been such an encouragement to my heart, knowing that no matter what I face, no matter what life throws at me, I will always have Jesus by my side.

Satan Wants What God Has

I didn't always know and grasp this truth. In my early

Christian walk, I went through a long struggle of doubt and shame, not understanding, at least in my heart, that when Jesus said that He had taken all of my sin, He literally meant all of it. There was nothing for me to feel guilty or ashamed about once Jesus had stepped in to take that away. It took six long years, but what I finally realized was that all of that shame and condemnation I was feeling, even after I had committed my life to Christ, was from the enemy.

Always keep in mind that Satan hates what God loves. He is always looking for a way to make us doubt, fear, or worry. He wants us living under the feeling of shame and condemnation, not the freedom that God promises. And the closer we get to Christ, the more Satan wants to tear us away. It is imperative that we cling to the verses above and realize that nothing Satan can do will separate us from Christ. He will never be more powerful than the love of Christ. Jesus' resurrection from the dead defeated Satan forever, and he cannot win.

He will definitely try, however. What Satan loves to do is find where we are most vulnerable and work on those areas. In my life, that has played out in my need for control. I don't mean that I feel like I need to control others' actions, but I do like to feel in control of the circumstances of my life. Even in the small things, like driving a car versus being a passenger, or the way the dishes or laundry are done, I have trouble giving control over to someone else.

My husband and kids like to joke that they don't like to load the dishwasher or fold the laundry because they know that I will just redo it. There is a running joke in my house about my actions in these areas, and it stems from the fact that I have often done just what they are joking about. Although it is not a matter of contention in my family, it is true, and it is something I have struggled with. While we as a family have been able to make light of it over the years, the part that is not funny is that often Satan has used it as an opportunity to make me feel like I've failed as a mother.

Because of my need to have things the way I want them and be in control, I haven't always made my kids do these kinds of chores. When I look at other families and see their seemingly perfect kids, I feel like I have somehow failed my own children. Allowing these thoughts to fester has turned into a vicious cycle in the past for me. When I would start to feel as if I failed my kids in one small area, I would begin to come up with other ways (real or imagined) that I wasn't the perfect mother to them. Before long, this rabbit trail would turn into other ways I felt inadequate. In what ways had I failed my husband? What areas of my job could I have done better? How many ways did I let God down today?

All of these were tactics that Satan used in my life to make me feel unlovable, like I could somehow be separated from the love of Christ, although Scripture told me that was impossible. Especially in my early Christian years, when I was already struggling with shame and self-doubt, this cycle of thinking happened often. I had very real fears that I would never be good enough; it seemed like everyone else had it all together except for me. I had a hard time figuring out how God could possibly love and use a mess-up like me.

Overcoming Doubt

It is in these moments or even seasons of doubt that it is vital to follow the example of Mary and sit at the feet of Jesus and learn from him. Before we will ever be able to serve Jesus well, we need to fully grasp the kind of love He has for us. It is a relentless love, one that will never let go. His love will never fail; it will remain forever.

Nothing you could ever do will mess you up so badly that He would leave your side. Once I really grasped this, my feelings of inadequacy melted away. I realized that my mistakes and shortcomings were actually part of my beautiful story of redemption through Jesus. I never would have found this love had I not sat at His feet and listened to Him.

I can't say that these feelings never creep back into my thought life. Just because I found healing doesn't mean it isn't still a weak area in my life that Satan still tries to use. The difference now is that I recognize this thought pattern. When these thoughts or feelings find their way back into my life, I am able to understand where they are coming from, take them captive, and give them over to Jesus (2 Corinthians 10:5). His perfect love takes care of it every time, and my weakness becomes strength through the power of Jesus Christ and His grace (2 Corinthians 12:9-10).

The Perfect Love of Christ

John chapter 17 has some of the most wonderful evidence of how much Jesus loves us. In this chapter of Scripture, we find Jesus praying to the Father just before He was arrested and crucified. Keep in mind that He knew exactly what was coming when He prayed these words. In verses 1-5, He prayed that God's glory would be revealed through Him. In verses 6-19, He prayed for His disciples. He prayed for their protection from the evil one and also that they would be unified. He prayed that they would have joy, even when the world hated them because of His name. He prayed for their sanctification as they went out into the world with His message.

Then, starting in verse 20, He prayed these words: "My prayer is not for them alone. I pray also for those who will believe in me through their message." Did you catch that? Jesus, knowing He was about to go to the cross, prayed for you. When I think about the kind of love shown here, it melts away any doubt I have that Jesus loves me fully, unconditionally, and eternally. If you read verses 21-23, He specifically prayed for unity among believers. Instead of being burdened by what He was about to suffer, He was burdened with love for His bride, the Church that would be born through the message about Him.

John 17:21 specifically portrays this love. Jesus said to the Father, "Just as you are in me and I am in you. May they also be in us so that the world may believe that you have sent me." Later, in verse 23, He prayed, "I in them and you in me." Jesus wants us to be wrapped up in Him, totally engulfed in His love, fully immersed in His presence. Realizing and understanding this requires us to sit at His feet. Then that understanding can turn into action—sharing His love with others.

Here are some other Scripture passages that can encourage your heart when you are in a time of wondering or doubting if the love of Jesus has left you. I have paraphrased each passage, but I encourage you to look up each one and meditate on the vast love of your Savior:

- Lamentations 3:22-23 – God's mercy is new every morning, and His great love ensures that we are not consumed by our sin.
- Isaiah 54:10 – God's love will never be shaken, no matter what might happen in the world around you.
- Psalm 86:15 – God is a God who does not get angry easily, He is very patient with us, and His love and faithfulness abound.
- 1 John 3:1 – God's love is lavished on us in the fact that He has adopted us as His children.
- 1 John 4:9-10 – God's love was on full display when He sent

His Son into the world to die for us so that we could live.

• 1 Chronicles 16:34 – God's love endures forever.

Works vs. Relationship

How does this all fit in with Mary and Martha? Think back on the entirety of the account of these two women and all of the things we have learned about our Christian walk throughout the previous chapters of this book. Recount the struggle Martha was going through as she served the Lord and got frustrated with her sister. Remember that Mary found what was better by sitting at the Lord's feet. Why was it better? It was the one thing that could not be taken away.

Your works, while they are important and necessary parts of your walk, are still temporary. The things you are able to do will change over time. As you age, you will find different interests and learn diverse ways of doing things. Your body also changes, making you unable to serve in some of the ways you were able to when you were younger.

Your relationship with the Lord, on the other hand, is eternal. While this relationship may change over time, it will not change in the same way your works do. Your works may fade away, but your connection to the Lord, if you nurture it, just gets more vivid. This is why it is so important to sit at His feet and learn from Him. The things you learn while sitting with Jesus can never be taken from you. Once you have found Him, He will always be with you. You have found what is better.

Moses' Example

Think again about the life of Moses that was discussed in chapter 4. Although he was by no means perfect, Moses spent a lot of time learning from the Lord. Many of these lessons were hard, but all of them matured him into the leader he would become. All of them were learned by sitting at the Lord's feet and, even when it was difficult, being obedient to Him. These were lasting lessons, truths that nobody could take away from Moses.

The first major encounter Moses had with God is found in Exodus chapters 3 and 4 in the scene at the burning bush. Although Moses didn't know at first that this strange sight was the Lord, once God introduced Himself, Moses had an unforgettable conversation with Him.

God was calling Moses to serve Him in a mighty way. While he was very reluctant about what God was asking him to do at first, we can see that by the end of the conversation, Moses found what was better. It was only by spending time with the Lord and learning from Him that Moses was able to complete the task set before him.

By sitting (or in the case of Moses, standing) at the Lord's feet, Moses was able to learn from God, understand God better, and gain strength for the journey to come. One of the first lessons Moses learned during this exchange was the patience and faithfulness of the Lord. Although Moses had numerous reasons why he was not the person to lead the Israelites out of Egyptian bondage, the Lord answered each of these reasons in the same manner: "I will be with you." God's answer was not always in these exact words, but each excuse of Moses was responded to with an assurance that he would not be on this journey alone.

It wasn't until the end of the exchange that Moses also learned that God's patience has limits. In Exodus 4:13, when Moses was able to see that his excuses and reasons for not serving weren't getting him anywhere, he said, "O Lord, please send someone else to do it." Up until this request, the Lord was very patient with Moses. However, in verse 14, we see that God had reached the point where He wanted Moses to just be obedient, and His "anger burned against Moses."

None of these important truths could have been grasped by Moses had he not taken the time to talk with the Lord. He could have realized that it was God in that burning bush and run away terrified, or he could have ignored the bush altogether. However, Moses made the conscious decision to stay, to spend valuable one-on-one time with God, and learn from Him. It wasn't all what he wanted to hear, it wasn't an easy conversation, but he stayed anyway.

When you read the rest of Exodus and see all of the incredible feats Moses was able to accomplish for the nation of Israel, it can all be traced back to this burning bush experience. The works that God did through Moses would not have been accomplished had it not been for the strength imparted when Moses spent time at the feet of the Lord. Moses found what was better, and it could not be taken from him. Those very first moments of interaction with God became part of his very being, and there was no force in heaven or on earth that could take that away.

Mary, Martha, and Us

So it was with Mary. She sat at the feet of Jesus, found what was better, and there was nothing that could take it away. I would love to hear the exchange between Mary and Martha right after Jesus left their home that day. I wonder if they talked about what Jesus meant by "what was better." I'm sure that both sisters learned a valuable lesson that day, and that both of them had something special they would treasure forever. We can have that same special truth. When we cling to what is better, it will not be taken from us.

Balance Your Mary and Martha

Sit at His Feet

Take your mind back to the passages of Scripture that were shared in this chapter. Spend some quiet time with the Lord contemplating the love of God that will never leave you. Allow Him to show you that His love will never fail.

Meditate on the following verses as you sit at His feet:

- Ephesians 3:17-19 – "That you may have power...to grasp how wide and long and high and deep is the love of Christ."
- 1 John 4:9-10 – "This is love: not that we loved God, but that he loved us." (v. 10)
- Romans 5:8 – "...While we were still sinners, Christ died for us."

Learn from Him

Take some time to think about and journal what you read in this chapter. Use the following questions to guide your thoughts.

- In what ways have you felt inadequate, like you could somehow have the love of Christ snatched away from you? How does Romans 8:38-39 encourage you in this area?
- How does it encourage your heart to know that Jesus prayed for you right before He was arrested and crucified?
- Notice that both Moses and Mary had to make the conscious decision to sit at the feet of the Lord and listen to Him. They could have chosen something else, but they chose what was better, and it could not be taken from them. What can you do to ensure that you make this decision every day?

Serve Him

Like Moses, allow what you learn in your quiet time with the Lord to stir you into action. Even if you are apprehensive about His call upon your life, take a step of faith and learn to serve Him. Since you have found what is better, take the next step and allow Him to work through you.

Put these passages of Scripture into practice as you serve Him:

- Ephesians 2:10 – "For we are God's handiwork, created in Christ Jesus to do good works, which God prepared in advance for us to do."

- Hebrews 13:20-21 – "Now may the God of peace...equip you with everything good for doing his will, and may he work in us what is pleasing to him, through Jesus Christ, to whom be glory for ever and ever. Amen."

- Hebrews 11:27 – "By faith [Moses] left Egypt, not fearing the king's anger; he persevered because he saw him who is invisible."

13

Time for Reflection

So many times in my life I have found that this balance between my Mary and Martha is difficult to find. On the surface it seems so simple—sit at the feet of Jesus and learn from Him, then go and put what you've learned into practice. However, the reality is that life is messy; life brings chaos that we never expect or anticipate. Even when there are no big problems in our lives, there are jobs, families, and other responsibilities that can get in the way of our quiet time and service.

It is my hope that, by taking an in-depth look at this account of Mary and Martha, we have learned some practical strategies for finding this balance. The challenge is to follow the pattern of both women. We need to make it a priority to have a divine appointment, to meet with Jesus every day, to sit at His feet and learn from Him. Just as important, we must find an area in which we can serve Him well. When this seems to be a struggle, it is time to revisit some of the strategies learned throughout these chapters. We should remember to lay aside the distractions that pull us away from our quiet time. Then, we must recognize what those distractions are and intentionally get them out of the room when we are spending time with the Lord.

Finally, it is important to acknowledge any obstacles that are getting in the way of our ability to hear from God. Is it awkward trying to talk to someone you can't see? Do you need to pick a better time of day in which you will be able to give the Lord your full attention?

In all of this, we need to be careful not to compare ourselves to others. Remember that these comparisons can cause us to either feel inadequate, or just the opposite, prideful. Neither of these thought patterns are healthy for the believer who wants to faithfully serve the Lord. We cannot allow our service become about recognition for ourselves or worrying about what others think about us.

Above all, it is my prayer that, by sitting at the Lord's feet, you will find the love of Christ and know that it can never be taken from you. When you, like Mary, find yourself immersed in His love, I hope you learn that nothing can separate you from Him.

I leave you with these benedictions from Scripture, encouragement written in the letters from Paul that you can take with you as you learn to sit at His feet and serve Him:

And now, dear children, continue in him, so that when he appears we may be confident and unashamed before him at his coming. If you know that he is righteous, you know that everyone who does what is right has been born of him (1 John 2:28-29).

Finally, brothers and sisters, whatever is true, whatever is noble, whatever is right, whatever is pure, whatever is lovely, whatever is admirable—if anything is excellent or praiseworthy—think about such things. Whatever you have learned or received or heard from me, or seen in me—put it into practice. And the God of peace will be with you (Philippians 4:8-9).

About the Author

BRENDA TROUTMAN is a Bible-believing Christian who desires to share with others what she has learned from Jesus in her own life. Brenda is married to her wonderful husband, Chris, and the two of them have three children together. She resides in Punxsutawney, Pennsylvania, the town that she has called home for her entire life. Brenda is a member of the Punxsutawney Christian and Missionary Alliance Church in Punxsutawney, Pennsylvania, where she serves on the worship team, teaches Sunday school, and serves as the Disciple Making Ministries Director.

She has also worked in Christian education for over twenty years, serving as a Bible, math, and science teacher. God called her to share her heart through writing, and she is so excited to see where this adventure will take her! It is her desire that others will grow in their relationship with Christ through reading what she has to share.

Use the following addresses to contact the author:
Email: brendatroutman86@gmail.com
Facebook: facebook.com/ouremmausjourney
Website: www.ouremmausjourney.com

www.ingramcontent.com/pod-product-compliance
Lightning Source LLC
Chambersburg PA
CBHW071156120626
46546CB00006B/2289